AYDA'S
ROAD

A Mother's Story for Her Children

PENIEL UNLIMITED, LLC
Michael and Kelly Marcades, Publishers
326 Valley Star Drive
Canyon Lake, Texas 78133
Website: http://www.penielunlimited.com
Email: michaelmarcades@gmail.com

PENIEL UNLIMITED, LLC . . . the "author's choice."

The vision of PENIEL UNLIMITED, LLC, as founded by Dr. Michael Glenn Marcades, President, and Kelly Marcades, CFO, is to provide superior publishing services for manuscripts worthy of public access. Since its inception, PENIEL UNLIMITED, LLC has taken a particular interest in manuscripts associated with, but not limited to, the assassination of President John F. Kennedy, choral music pedagogy, children's literature, faith-based books, and more.

Printed in the United States of America
Copyright © 2025, Ayda Lydia Escamilla
ISBN: 979-8-218-73975-1

Book Cover Design & Production by Daniel Whisnant
(www.suissemade.com)
10 9 8 7 6 5 4 3 2

AYDA'S
ROAD

A Mother's Story for Her Children

by Ayda Lydia Escamilla

Editor: Michael Glenn Marcades, PhD
Published 2025 PENIEL UNLIMITED, LLC

AYDA'S ROAD
A Mother's Story for Her Children

—

CONTENTS

One of the unique benefits of the publishing industry is the opportunity to be involved in the lives of authors worldwide through the intense editing and formatting processes of their approved manuscript submissions. In many cases, authors have devoted years, even decades, to associated research and writing. In and of itself, the author's act of sharing their final manuscript with a potential publisher, and later with a worldwide readership, takes courage.

The following narrative, AYDA'S ROAD, is a mother's tale that embodies themes of love, courage, persistence, and hope. Ayda's journey, as a wife, mother, sister, and friend to many, is like many untold life stories. It is one of joy, sadness, celebration, occasional regret, and faith in the one and only God, who never abandons His people. This book chronicles Ayda's life from childhood to the present day, capturing the essence of her experiences and the lessons she learned along the way.

July 2025 – PENIEL UNLIMITED, LLC
Dr. Michael Marcades – President, Executive Editor
Kelly Casey Marcades – CFO, Technology and
Marketing Director

MEET THE AUTHOR: *Ayda Lydia Escamilla*

Ayda Lydia Escamilla has walked a life path that is uniquely hers. Her journey, like those of many women, has included twists and turns due to life circumstances. She loved without reservation, including six husbands, five children (all now grown with families of their own), ten grandchildren, six great-grandchildren, and a host of friends across seven decades.

Ayda's expansive ancestral roots include men and women who came to America from Italy, Portugal, Spain, Mexico, and the Aztec regions of Central Mexico. Some of her ancestors endured the Battle of the Alamo, while others survived life challenges dating back to the 16th century.

As a woman, *Ayda* endured abuse at the hands of some who claimed to love her. Not one to easily give up, *Ayda*, in the face of childhood poverty and limited life opportunities, relentlessly pursued formal education, which facilitated a successful four-decade career in nursing. *Ayda*, now seventy-five years old, has retired from nursing and spends her days enjoying true love with her husband, Jose Abreo Acosta, caring for their home, and attending to the needs of her family.

AYDA'S ROAD, a journey worth discovering.

IN MEMORIA

With gratitude and love to my mother
MARIA YSABEL MUNIZ DE ESCAMILLA

—

DEDICATED TO MY CHILDREN

Annette
Salvador Jr.
Thelma
Ada Stephanie
Nina

CHAPTER ONE: *Childhood to August 2000*

I was just four years old when Julio, my nine-year-old brother, died. That day was etched in my mind forever. My parents' house overflowed with people paying their respects and offering comfort wherever possible. As expected, sadness blanketed our family. My mother was visibly distraught; at times, her grief was so heavy that she collapsed on the floor and rolled over and over in front of everyone. Though understandable, her behavior scared all of us, particularly me.

In the following years, Mother spoke about Julio as if he were still living. From time to time, she would openly talk to him out loud. "Eugenia Reyes was drunk when she killed you! All because she decided to pass a truck to see the driver!" Mother's anger and grief frequently spewed out of her mouth.

Throughout my childhood, my parents fought a lot, for reasons that escaped me. Although I knew they loved each other, their arguing always scared me, so much that I tried to hide it from my sister Belia.

As I grew older, I learned a great deal about my parents, including how they met and got married. Mom first caught Dad's eye while riding her bicycle in the street. Dad was twelve years older, more mature, and confident. Determined to meet this young beauty, Dad approached and introduced himself; the encounter scared her so much that she hastily rode off to her sister's house.

Later, Mom went to a local carnival with some friends. While there, her stockings fell to her ankles because she did not have "stocking holders." As she bent over to pull up her stockings, Dad, who was standing nearby, saw the whole scene. He walked closer and teasingly said, "I see you are interested in me!" Once again, Dad's approach scared her, yet this time she managed to pull herself together enough to respond. "I'm only trying to fix it because I can't afford holders. I'm NOT trying to sell myself!"

Sometime later, five men, along with my grandfather, came to my aunt's house and asked for my mother's hand in marriage. In September 1927, my mother, Maria Ysabel Muniz, was only fourteen when she married my father, Luis Lopez Escamilla.

Early in my parents' marriage, my dad worked as a butcher at Nester's, a local supermarket, and sold meat all over Hondo. In those days, he sold small and large pans of meat for $0.25 and $0.50, respectively. (Mother didn't work until after Dad died. Her employment life was diverse; she was a nurse's aide, salesclerk, seamstress, custom knitter, and quilt maker.)

For reasons I didn't fully understand, Dad gambled away some of his pocket money. On good nights, after we kids were on the scene, he'd come home with pockets full of change. Mary, Belia, and I loved counting the coins. If we were lucky, Dad would reward us with a few dimes, "chivas" as he called them.

I was born on Father's Day at Hondo Memorial Hospital in Hondo, Texas, a small town west of San Antonio. At that time, Hondo didn't have ambulance service. As a result, the funeral home staff transported me home in a hearse. Unlike today, early 20th-century doctors usually required all new mothers to remain in bed for six weeks! (For the record, Mom was never given her father's name because my grandmother never had the opportunity to marry Mr. Muniz. Maria Eufrosina Navarro Rivera died prematurely of tuberculosis at the age of forty-two. Consequently, I don't carry his name either, while my brothers all carry the Muniz name.)

Both my parents were proud natives of Mexico. Mom was born in Masapil, Zacatecas, Mexico, and Dad was born in Zaragosa, Coahuila, the northern portion of Mexico. (Those familiar with this northern region know it as the "birthplace" of Tejano / "Texas" music.) Later in life, Mom and Dad paid the price to become legal citizens of the United States of America; in no way were they "wetbacks." In their minds, they became proud "Tejanos."

Spanish was our family's primary language. (Unfortunately, I have forgotten most of what I knew as a child.) Having Spanish as my "first" language complicated my learning to speak English. I remember failing first grade, simply because my English skills were not strong. I was so confused that I even misunderstood how to spell my first name, Ayda. For quite some time, I thought it was spelled Ida! Although I speak English fluently now, the "English road" was a tough one.

Life in Hondo, Texas, was unique. Everyone knew everyone else; honestly, it seemed everyone was related! Our immediate and extended families grew; cousins, brothers, sisters, and friends were everywhere. As one big family, we cooked our food and created music that was a marvelous mixture of Mexican and Texan traditions.

My family was quite large; I had five brothers (Luis Fidencio, Juan, Efrain, Oscar, and Julio) and five sisters (Clotilde, also known as Tillie, Elia Juiett, Sofia, and Belia Guadalope), plus my niece, Mary. (My parents raised Mary from the day she was two weeks old.) We were a close-knit group, always looking out for each other.

We all lived in a two-bedroom house with an outside restroom. Times were hard. Nevertheless, we managed to care for a variety of animals, including goats, calves, chickens, ducks, cats, and dogs.

As one might expect, we experienced a lot on "the farm." I remember when one of the calves pinned down my baby sister Belia on the ground. Instinctively, I ran to my mom for help. I was terrified that she was going to die. Another time, Mary, always getting into trouble, fell into the outside toilet. Again, I asked my mom for help. (It took a lot of soap to clean her!) Mary also got her arms caught in our old washer wringers. Of course, like most kids, Mary was prone to falling from trees.

I had my share of childhood mishaps. One day, my sister Sofie and my brother Oscar grabbed me by the feet, smashed and twisted my head. Mom rushed me to Dr. Mims. I remember that I screamed when he returned my head to its normal position. It hurt plenty!

Despite the challenges of growing up in a large family, I was surrounded by love and support. My siblings, close friends, and I were unaware of our parents' financial struggles. We all loved our homes and schools. My friendships with Belia Gonzales, Delia Ramirez, Martha Rodriguez, Martha Correa, and Ester Correa were a source of joy and laughter, even on rainy days when we joked about being from *"el borrio de la rana,"* a neighborhood of frogs!

During summer breaks, I spent a lot of time with my older sisters, Tillie Clothilde and Elia Juliet, and friends, who were *like* family to me. All three girls were married in my teenage years, and the responsibilities of marriage limited our time together. Now and then, there were group outings to the Hondo movie theater, which cost only $0.25. Those experiences helped break summer boredom. Fortunately, because of her great love and for my good, my mom kept close tabs on me.

Despite the loneliness, I was still a reasonably happy person.

Spanish families commemorate a girl's fifteenth birthday with a Quinceañera Party. Mom and Dad made sure that mine was remarkable. Fourteen of my girlfriends were present. And my brother, Efrain Escamilla, and his group, "Las Agilas de Tejas," provided vocal and instrumental entertainment that was enjoyed by all. (Efrain's group often performed at weddings and dance halls. Income from these events helped him and his wife, Mary, raise nine children.)

My father died of lung cancer when I was sixteen. His death made me angry, so much so that I could not shed a grieving tear. In desperation, I sought consolation, comfort, and security in my boyfriend, Salvador Dominguez Leyva. It wasn't long before we were married on August 5, 1967, at Our Lady of Guadalupe Roman Catholic Church. Over 300 people received invitations to the wedding ceremony. Father Robert Silverman presided. My wedding party consisted of six married women, who served as godmothers and witnesses, and six single girlfriends, who represented the roses. The wedding was beautiful, and I felt like Cinderella.

July 15, 2000

As with all new marriages, Sal and I were learning what it meant to love and care for each other day after day. Naturally, we had our ups and downs, but the first year of marriage seemed "normal." Frequently, Sal and I danced and partied away the evening hours. Sal's parents, Ventura and Juanita Leyva, owned a bar in Hondo called "Leyva's Bar." As owners, Ventura and Juanita were always very busy; he managed the bar while she managed the restaurant. Periodically, Ventura and Juanita called Sal to help with the business when things got busy at the bar. (Unfortunately, that did not bring money into our household. Sal worked for free.)

Early on, I became pregnant. After a few months of just staying home, I became bored. Because I had only completed eighth grade, my poor mother encouraged me to finish my education. Eventually, I broached the possibility of returning to school with Sal. For some reason, he wasn't keen on the idea; honestly, I believed he was jealous and threatened by my love of learning and desire to better myself. Habitually, Sal prioritized his needs over mine.

On July 30, 1968, I went into labor and delivered a beautiful baby girl; I named her Annette Marie. (I wanted a name like Virgin Mary, but not Maria.)

As time passed, I became dissatisfied with living a "normal" life; I wanted more. Sal, though employed, was content with small jobs. Then, he landed a job at a local print shop; he learned to repair and maintain typewriters. Initially, his work went well, and he developed good skills. Then, out of the blue, he lost confidence in himself. Almost every day, he suffered from unexplainable, rattled nerves. It wasn't long before his emotional state led to severe, rather debilitating panic attacks. He increasingly became unable to drive somewhere on his own. Almost always, I had to drive him everywhere. I quickly tired of having to do so.

Mounting stresses between Sal and me took a heavy toll on our marriage. In 1969, we processed our first divorce. (Yes, remarriage was in our future.) Despite the divorce, we continued seeing each other. I still loved him. Deep inside, I knew he was smart, as evidenced by his graduation from high school with straight A's. I had every confidence that he could be successful in life.

In February 1970, I went out on a date. That night, I got pregnant. One year earlier, I lost a baby, and I certainly didn't want to lose another. After I became pregnant, Sal and I decided to try marriage again.

Sadly, nothing changed. We argued and fought regularly over many things, including the fact that Sal insisted I not be around his friends. When we married, I was aware that he was a party animal. His demand that I not be around his friends made me suspicious. What did he wish to hide? Was he embarrassed to have his wife by his side? Nevertheless, I chose to see Sal in positive ways. I firmly believed that he was a good, fully capable of being a strong father and family man.

In late fall 1970, I gave birth to a son, whom we named Sonny. (I was determined to select a name better than Salvador!) Much to our surprise, Sonny had blue eyes. Immediately, Sal declared that Sonny was not his child. He suspected that Dr. Zigenbalg, my blue-eyed boss, was the father. As the doctor's office nurse, everyone respected and liked me. Consequently, those who knew me well hated Sal for his accusation.

Two weeks after Sonny was born, I returned to work. Thankfully, my mother and mother-in-law (who owned her own business) took turns caring for their grandson while I worked. While I was grateful for their loving, sacrificial help, I was concerned that they would get exhausted. Caring for a newborn is a demanding responsibility, even for a young and resilient mother. These loving women were older and had long since stopped caring for newborns. Yet, they helped.

After having just had a child, I chose to wear an intrauterine device as a means of preventing untimely pregnancies. However, just two months later, I experienced early pregnancy symptoms, including nausea and vomiting. One way or the other, I had to know whether I was pregnant again.

A short time later, I asked my boss, Dr. Zigenbalg, to perform a pelvic exam. The doctor's exam confirmed that I was two months pregnant with my third child. Once again, Sal's and my genetic combination produced a beautiful, very white, blue-eyed girl whom I named Thelma. (Thelma's eye color changed as she matured.)

Initially, Sal acted as if he were pleased with the children. However, little time passed before his friends were his priority. More frequently, Sal resorted to the old habit of going out alone with his friends, leaving me to do most of the tedious parenting on my own.

Soon, our daily life was again filled with one argument or fight after another. This time, my patience ran out much faster than the last time. I gave up trying, which led to our second divorce in 1975.

Again, and perhaps against our better judgment, we agreed to get back together in late 1975 / early 1976. Determined to mitigate another untimely pregnancy, I took birth control pills. Nevertheless, another pregnancy followed; we were blessed with another girl whom we named Stephanie, after Estefana de Leyva, Sal's grandmother. Still, Sal and I struggled to love and care for each other well. Fights continued to be a regular part of our daily lives.

July 17, 2000

I remember the summer of 1971 as if it were just yesterday. One night, Sal stumbled into the house around 3:00 a.m. As providence would have it, I had seen him pick up a girl that evening, so I assumed he had been with her.

As Sal entered the house, I jumped out of bed to meet him. What ensued was nothing short of all-out war.

"Have you been seeing someone behind my back?" he shouted.

"Yes!" I yelled back.

Sal had asked whether he was our son's father for two years. I angrily replied, "Yes, I have been seeing someone. And... you aren't the father of our son!"

I was weary of Sal's doubting whether he was our son's father. In the heat of the moment, I decided he wanted to hear the worst, so I lied.

"My son never belonged to you! Finally, you get the truth you've wanted to hear for over two years!"

As soon as the words left my mouth, I realized I had made a terrible mistake. But it was too late. Sal erupted. I thought he was going to kill my son and me. And, in utter defiance, he went out with my nieces!

Looking back on Stephanie's birth, I'm reminded how much she favored Sal. I hoped this child would make him a happy and contented husband and father. Sadly, I was hoping against hope. Believe it or not, Sal took his infidelity to an even higher level by dating multiple women. He even tried to date some of my relatives.

Even after all this time, I still marveled at Sal's behavior. Not only was he stupid, but he was also abusive. Near the end, he beat me up so badly that I had to get immediate medical care. As a result, photos of my injuries were taken and passed along to a divorce lawyer. Moreover, Salvador lied to my children about me being a witch! (Apparently, he misunderstood my constant efforts to love and care for those around me. If I HAD been a witch, I would have said "Poof!" and made him disappear! In all seriousness, He must have been sick.) With good reason, I divorced Salvador in 1977.

Looking back on my life with my parents, I recall being taught that the man is always right in marriage and that the woman must do whatever is necessary to make it work. That entire marriage lesson was hard for me to swallow at this point in life.

As I wrestled with the situation, I sought guidance from others, including my attorney, Clyde Haake. To avoid upsetting her, I kept my mom out of it; she had enough to worry about caring for my sister, Belia.

At one point, in absolute desperation, I sought the advice of Curandera, a self-declared witch doctor. This entire venture was a waste of time; she didn't tell me anything I did not already know.

"Leave him, and above all, stay ahead of him or he will kill you!" exclaimed Curandera.

Even my priest agreed by saying, "I told you so!"

Like many young women, I grew up fast. Tough decisions confronted me from the very beginning. I responded well to these challenges; I became a nurse and managed a retail store in Hondo for five years. Eventually, after divorcing Sal, I bought the place and called it Lydia's Apparel.

Yet, few of my accomplishments and tenacity served me well. People always chimed in with their judgmental opinions and actions. Even Sal's parents, the Leyvas, refused to let me live a normal life. Astoundingly, they threatened me and spread lies about me everywhere.

Then, out of the blue, amongst all the negativity, I met Albert Joe Lovato one day at the store. As we talked about all that was going on between me and Sal, he said:

"Ayda, we all know Sal; he's never thought of anyone but himself, and if you make him angry, he retaliates. Let's face it, he can be a vindictive, harsh man." Finally, someone was on my side. (Little did I know how much Albert's connection would impact me.)

As I looked back on my time with Sal, I was reminded that I knew what I was getting into when I fell in love; the whole process led me to ignore many things. Sadly, my passion for Sal had made me emotionally blind. Over and over, I hoped that the arguing would stop, that he would be happy after our children were born, and that he would love me more than anyone else.

Years passed before things became clear; believe me, I had seen and heard plenty. His lies led me to lie. *"I guess this is what he needs and prefers. He was born into a house of lies. To Sal, lying was as normal as taking a breath."* Before we divorced, these thoughts kept running through my mind again. But now, I am free. Never again.

As I faced the future, I thought about Albert. His caring actions toward me captivated me. He was an extraordinary man who had endured his share of pain and disappointment. His former wife cheated on him. According to Albert, he caught his ex-wife with another man. I knew that Albert loved his wife greatly. At times, I pondered whether he would love me as much. As time passed, I reveled in his respectful, gentlemanly treatment of me and my children. That alone was enough to make me fall in love with him.

We were married on January 2, 1979, and moved to Marlin, Texas. A little over a year later, on March 11, 1980, I gave birth to a daughter. We named her Nina Ruby.

Somewhat unexpectedly, our time in Marlin was brief. Albert, now employed by Pizza Hut, was transferred to Nebraska. While we were there, I attended college to pursue a career in nursing, and Albert took auto mechanic classes on the side. Unlike myself, Annette, Albert's stepdaughter, was unhappy in the Midwest. Consequently, we returned to Texas in November 1982. Our children's happiness mattered. *(Additional details provided under July 30, 2000.)*

Unfortunately, we returned to the same family problems we had left, primarily issues with Sal and Delia Nira, Albert's ex-wife. Delia Nira and Albert shared a daughter, Tina Marie Lovato. Initially, Albert was allowed to see Tina when I was absent. Seeing Tina was important to me, and I never gave up looking for ways to be with her. Eventually, I was successful. (Long ago, and for many years, Delia Nira and I attended school together. I have known Tina since she was a baby. Often, her grandmother brought her shopping at my store.)

Being back in Texas was chaotic due to family issues. As soon as we returned, Delia filed for child support. She could not secure substantial support because I had five children living under our roof. Nevertheless, she continued to pursue an increase in child support. (All in all, she made our lives very difficult. Though I could not prove it, I suspected she and Sal were maintaining a relationship.)

From 1985 to 1990, my life was in utter chaos. Every time I pursued taking Sal to court for one reason or another, Delia did the same with Albert. The pressure from this situation was unbearable. I remember singing in the church choir as a means of relief. Occasionally, I talked to different people about what was happening.

By the end of 1985, I knew my marriage was falling apart. Problems kept getting bigger and bigger. At times, it seemed as if God was not listening to me. In desperation, I just gave up and pushed Albert toward divorce.

July 23, 2000

My children visited me today; their presence made this Sunday even more special. It's late now, and my thoughts wander. Many years have passed, yet I still vividly remember the days I spent with Mom in her small house. I was utterly fascinated by stories from her past.

There are many tales of my family roots and diverse history. My paternal grandparents came to America from Europe, and my grandfather's parents were of Greek and Italian descent. Back then, the name "Escamilla" was spelled "Escamillo."

Grandfather Cristino Escamilla was born in San Antonio, Mexico. Before the Battle of the Alamo, he was taken to Northern Mexico for his safety; doing so probably saved his life. (Sadly, his mother was killed by hanging in the present-day park immediately in front of Santa Rosa Hospital.) Grandfather Cristino grew up in Northern Mexico. He met and eventually married Maria Del Pilar López, whose parents were from Spain. Maria's skin was light and fair, and her eyes were deep blue, like the sea. Conversely, Cristino's skin resembled that of dark-skinned Greeks.

Maria came from a wealthy family that owned extensive land in Piedras Negras, Mexico. (In fact, buildings on that land are still present today. As you enter Mexico from Texas, these pink-colored buildings are visible. They belonged to my grandmother, Maria del Pilar. Unfortunately, my grandfather tricked her into selling off the land. In the process, she was coerced into signing documents that she did not understand. Everything was lost.)

My great-grandfather, Petronilo Escamilla, was at the Alamo in 1835, just before the battle started. According to family folklore, he spent a considerable amount of time with a Cherokee medicine man at the Alamo.

Many of my relatives live in Zaragosa, Rosita, Aguas Calientes, and Piedras Negras, Coahuila, Mexico. Other locations include:

- Guadalupe Escamilla (a lawyer) and Héctor Escamilla (a physician) who presently live in San Antonio, Texas
- Mr. Muniz, whose first name is unknown to me, my mother's father, lived in Masapil, Zacatecas, Mexico, near Mexico City. (He worked in the silver mines and died before my mother was born.)

Maria Juanita Navarro was my great-grandmother. She was of Spanish descent, with blue-green eyes and light skin. She married Jose Rivera, an Aztec Indian.

My maternal grandmother, Maria Eufrosina Navarro Rivera, who bore a resemblance to her father, grew up in Masapil. She and my mother were quite resourceful. They did whatever was necessary to earn money and survive in the world.

People knew Maria as a midwife, a healer, and a "card" reader, a practice my mother continued in later life. (Historically, card reading, or tarot reading, was a practice where an individual used a deck of tarot cards to gain insights or answer questions regarding a person's life.) Grandmother warned that tarot reading took practice, but once mastered, it protected her and others from the casual world. Perhaps she sensed that she would not live much longer.

My grandmother's life was unique, to say the least. In 1921, she hitched up a one-horse wagon and fled to Hondo, Texas, with my mother in tow. Fortunately, the two of them were not alone. Instead, they were joined by others from Mexico. (On the journey, Grandmother wore dense, long skirts; underneath, she hid fully loaded pistols which she was fully prepared to use.) Providentially, the extended family waited for them in Hondo; my aunt, Bonefacia Benavides, and her husband, Isidro, had already lived there. The fact that Aunt Bonefacia was Mother's half-sister didn't compromise the family connection. Family is family.

July 30, 2000

Today, my first daughter, Annette Leyva Wagner, turned 32! Impossible! I just returned from a well-attended celebration at her house. Everyone was there, including my sister, Juliette Morales; my husband, Albert; Stephanie; Katherine Marie; and Jesse Alexander. During the party, I noticed Annette's baby book on the table; thumbing through the pages brought a flood of memories. Immediately, Maria del Refugio Griego, my great-grandmother, came to mind. This is a woman of great accomplishment and courage. Sadly, she was hanged by a white man right after giving birth to a baby boy (my future grandfather) during the 1835 Alamo battle in San Antonio. Her name may be etched in stone on an Alamo-related monument in Washington, D.C.; if you are ever there, look and see.

As we partied, we all shared stories about the past and fond memories. Tillie and I relived driving for the first time; I was only 9 years old when our parents introduced us to driving! (*"Never too young to start learning"* was Mother's attitude about learning almost anything.) Most of the time,

Mom and Dad also let my sister Tillie teach us. I was so small that I couldn't see above the steering wheel. Not to be deterred, I just peeked through the wheel opening. Such fun!

As a young girl, I always envied what my older sisters did, and I was anxious to do the same things. Earning money was one of the things I envied. I talked about it so much that Mother let me drop out of school when I was eleven, so I could clean the houses of wealthy people. In those days, I cleaned houses for $12.00 a week. Every payday, I gave Mom $10.00 and kept $2.00. Eventually, that working arrangement fell by the wayside, and I returned to school as a sixth grader. Much to my dismay, I failed that year. The following year, I returned and did well until I met Salvador. In short order, we got married, and although I wanted to, I didn't go back to school.

In February 1980, I completed and passed the Texas High School Equivalency Examination. One month later, Nina Ruby Lovato was born on March 11, 1980. A few days later, on March 23, 1980, I went to Waco to receive an original copy of my GED diploma. I felt good about myself; I gave birth and graduated from high school!

This emotional high was short-lived. Unexpectedly, Pizza Hut transferred Albert to Lyman, Nebraska. To move, we were forced to sell our four-bedroom home, a decision I soon regretted greatly.

Once in Lyman, Albert and I were both allowed to attend Western Nebraska College. He pursued auto mechanics, and

I was thrilled to attend nursing school. As luck would have it, severe financial difficulties quickly overshadowed this positive development. Our finances were stretched thin, and I couldn't support my children. As a result, I was forced to apply for and receive Medicaid, as well as other state-supported assistance. And, as if we needed more problems, our beautiful children were miserable in Nebraska. For their sake, we gladly returned to Texas.

In September 1982, Albert returned to work at Pizza Hut, and we moved to Schertz, Texas. Returning to Texas brought good and bad things into our lives. Irreversible impacts and decisions were made:

> First, relocating to Texas erased ten months of nursing credits accrued in Nebraska—ten months lost! Undeterred, I returned to nursing school in Texas and graduated as a fully Licensed Vocational Nurse (LVN) on February 28, 1984.

> Second, I decided to divorce Albert. In retrospect, doing so proved to be a terrible mistake. Some of our happiest years were in Schertz. Mistakenly, I convinced myself that life was horrible, but looking back, things weren't so bad. We should have gone to marriage counseling. Nevertheless, when all was said and done, we divorced.

> And thirdly, I married David Tristan on the rebound. On reflection, while I liked David, I certainly did not love him. And I suspected that he was involved in some form of witchcraft. At my insistence, our

marriage, which had lasted less than thirty days, was annulled and erased from all court records in July 1992.

I launched my nursing career at Universal City Minor Emergency Center, owned by Dr. Richard Park. Naturally, he inquired about my previous nursing experience. "I was at Hondo Memorial Hospital in 1968, then later I worked with Dr. Ziegenbalg in Castroville, Texas," I said proudly.

Dr. Park was an experienced military doctor but had little experience working alone. Early on, a patient entered the clinic with a head injury; he was bleeding extensively. Oddly, Dr. Park had no idea how to stop the bleeding. And he was letting his nerves get the best of him.

Determined to help, I instructed him to locate a small vein and tie a knot with 4-0 nylon cord. It was as if my words fell on deaf ears. So, I said, "Take a short break, gather yourself, and come back in a minute."

After a few minutes, Dr. Park returned, stopped the bleeding, and processed the necessary stitches as if it were the most natural thing in the world. After we released the patient, Dr. Park complimented me on how I handled myself. "She's a great nurse!" he declared. As a young nurse, his words meant the world to me. I love my career. (I guess nursing was in my blood. My dad's father and mom's mother were midwives; they delivered many babies. My grandfather even wanted to deliver my mom's first son. Mom had something to say about that; he didn't deliver that boy!)

Today, I remember many things about growing up in my parents' house. As a child, my sisters, Tillie, Elia, Sofie, and my brother, Oscar, still lived at home. My older brothers were already married, and my sisters always worked while I was in school. Day after day, I walked there and back. Then, amazingly, a lady from the Barrio de las Ranas, a poor neighborhood in Hondo, bought a small, ten-passenger bus. From that point forward, I rode the bus; lucky me. Later, Mary and Belia also rode the bus.

For as long as I can remember, our house was filled with music. Music made me happy. My brother Efrain had his band, Mom loved to sing, Dad loved Country and Western music, and he was quite a dancer. We frequently went dancing with friends, including the Hernandez family. It was always fun. As I approached dating, my parents always encouraged me to *dance* at the dance, rather than drinking alcohol until I looked and behaved ridiculously.

Early on, Dad taught me all the best dance moves. I became a dancing fool! Not only did I love it, but it was good exercise. "Dance, dance, dance!" was my motto. As you'd expect, Dad kept an eye on me at dances. When I was fifteen, he was highly protective. I was not allowed to dance with guys, especially not older men. Of course, eventually I WAS allowed to dance with approved guys. Even then, I could tell that he was jealous.

As a ten-year-old Junior High School student, I had the opportunity to study piano with Clemencia Gonzales, Mom's close friend, who lived in Hondo, Texas. Taking piano lessons with Mrs. Gonzales was a special privilege. In time, I learned that her life was filled with pain. Her husband beat her mercilessly, so hard that she went partially blind in one eye.

I usually walked home after lessons. About halfway back, I always broke into a hard sprint. (Generally speaking, Hondo was a safe town. However, drunk drivers who drove too fast frequently ended up in our front yard. Finally, Mom put up a substantial fence, and that was the end of that! It's still there.)

Meeting Clemencia's daughter, Belia Gonzales, was a side blessing, in addition to studying piano. She became one of my closest friends. Our friendship has endured to this day. Belia was much more than just a friend; she was loyal. In her mind, and I realize she was probably biased; I've never done anything wrong. And I certainly don't need to hang my head in shame about anything. Calling her a "true friend" doesn't quite cover it. I loved her dearly. Belia, Simona Correa, and I played together regularly. Times were so hard that we had to have fun wherever we could. Sometimes, after we cleaned them by smashing them with our bare feet, we frolicked in mom's wet sheets hanging outside.

1992 was an eventful year that started with my move to New Braunfels, Texas. Most people thought all was well, and I was having a great time living there. WRONG! This time frame was some of the worst years of my life.

Most of my children weren't happy with me. I tried desperately to have a good relationship with Nina, but she clearly could not stand me. (No one had to tell me this; a mother knows.) Stephanie tried to make things better, but to no avail. And if that were not enough, finances were horrible.

There was no money for food or the most basic bills. One terrible, dead-of-winter night, life hit rock bottom. There was no electricity or heat, and the temperature inside our house was the same as outside. We were cold and void of hope. As Stephanie and I held each other, tears rolled down our faces.

The next day, I went to the grocery store. I placed badly needed food items into the grocery cart one by one. I knew full well that I didn't have the money to pay for everything. Nevertheless, I wrote a check and handed it to the cashier. By the next day, my check bounced at the bank. The nightmare continued. Beyond belief, I was arrested for writing a hot check. I spent that night behind bars. Never had I been more humiliated.

Risking everything, I summoned the courage to ask Barbara Gerth, a coworker, to help me cover the bounced check and fees. The desperation I felt as she laughed in my face was beyond description. My heart sank to a new low. No friends. No money. Yet, I found some comfort in the fact that I was a certified nurse. I'd find work somewhere else. Clearly, I needed to put New Braunfels behind me.

Life was crashing down all around. No hope anywhere. I even thought about killing myself. My children hated me, and I feared that our relationship might be forever lost. What could be more devastating to a mother than separation from her children? Even now, right now, I can't help but cry when I remember the pain and anguish that blanketed my life then. I pray that my children will never feel such hopelessness or be forced to do anything and everything to merely survive life.

Annette, Sonny, Thelma, Stephanie, and Nina – I LOVE YOU DEEPLY.

In 1993, a ray of light and hope entered my life. I met John Albert Bermea at a dance hall called T-Town. Our initial connection came quite naturally; our eyes met, and mutual smiles conveyed mutual interest. Those brief moments marked the beginning of our love affair, or whatever you want to call it. Miraculously, John knew exactly what I went through in New Braunfels, and he promised to take care of me and Stephanie. He insisted that we marry. After all I had been through, I wasn't sure about marriage. Determined to move on in life with a new beginning, I set aside my hesitant feelings. We got married on August 7, 1993, at La Villita.

The ceremony was simple yet lovely. Mom and my sister Juliette attended. Once again, I felt a return of lost feelings of happiness and hope inside me. (John rescued me from

New Braunfels at a hopeless time. I believe I would be dead now if it weren't for him. And even though my children weren't happy about everything, my heart soared. Life was great, great, great.

As time passed, John became extremely loving and supportive. His only negative trait was that he didn't like kids. (His mother and sister felt the same way, so his position was understandable.)

After five wonderful years, John left me, ending our marriage. Though I will never return to him, I will love and remember him for the rest of my life. Up to this point in my life, John was the only husband who treated me respectfully and cared for me. (Lesson learned: never go back to someone who leaves you!)

May God bless all my husbands; only the Lord knows what they need. Besides, everything happens for a reason. In the process, I sought forgiveness from Albert J. Lovato, whom I later married on September 28, 1999.

Albert and I get along very well. (Not hating each other surely helps!) We care for each other deeply, and our daughter, Nina, means the world to us. We love her beyond description and never wish to hurt her again.

To my children, I say: Albert cares deeply for all of you. And . . . he loves me. That proves a lot to me as your mother and his wife. Please, forever respect him. Without him, we probably wouldn't be here enjoying life.

CHAPTER TWO: *2000-2001*

August 2, 2000

Yesterday was Katherine Marie Correa's birthday. Katherine is a deep part of me now and will forever be. I wasn't about to let her birthday pass without talking to her. As I suspected, her grandmother, Chavela, didn't want me to speak to Katherine. Chavela's desire to control and manipulate my friendship and communication with Katherine always angers me, but this time, it pushed me exceptionally hard. Fortunately, I resisted lashing out at her. Doing so took every ounce of self-control that I could muster.

I believe that Katherine and her mom will eventually come around and see the truth about everything. And I don't think anything could permanently damage the love between Katherine and Annette Marie. As for me, I hear and understand everything that's being said; I'm not deaf! People always "talk" without fully understanding situations. Unlike many, Annette exercises wisdom beyond her age. No person knows everything; only God sees all the "whys" and "wheres." Even then, God forgives everything, and we should do likewise.

Despite life's difficulties, I have faith in the Lord. Slowly but surely, I believe he will return all my flock. To all, I say: may we all learn the truth and live better lives. But in the final analysis, everything, yes everything, is in God's hands.

I don't have much else on my mind today, apart from the fact that I want all of you, regardless of where you are in this world, near or far away, to know that you are NEVER forgotten. I love you all. May God bless you beyond your imagination.

August 30, 2000

Albert and I just returned from a wonderful family reunion in Longmont, Colorado. However, our enjoyment was dampened by the absence of my children and Ruby and Lloyd Lovato. Inside, I felt deeply depressed. I know that life always "goes on," but it was almost more than I could bear right now.

This morning, I woke up to deafening silence at home. It's funny how a mother revels in the daily household noise of raising children; honestly, the chaos was heavenly for me. Once the kids grew up, I struggled to accept their absence. Nothing replaces that feeling of loss. And on top of it all, at Albert's insistence, I'm forced to tell my grown kids that they can't stay here. Inside, there are no words. Pushing them away breaks my heart, most especially when it comes to Sonny or Stephanie. I love them beyond description. I pray that someday they will understand. But now, in the present, I beg God to shield them from the temptation of drugs. Drugs... a one-way ticket to death.

Fortunately, I'm on vacation from work; it's nice to be off for two weeks. Thanks to arthritis, every day is filled with pain. (*You'd think being a nurse would help me eliminate the hurt!*) Not fun at all. I must hurry up and get rich to "catch up with the Joneses!" Then, I'll walk away from the grind and enjoy life.

Looking back, things are so different now than when I was growing up. Day after day, I do all I can to survive in life. Everything is so damn expensive—no cable; hell, not much of anything extra. Life is a struggle. It all makes me very sad. And who knows how much longer we'll all be here. The 80s flew by, and the 90s seem out of reach. I may not even live that long. Whatever comes, comes. Life has its way: "Here today, gone tomorrow."

No more words for today; only deep love for my entire family.

October 7, 2000

Thinking a lot about my mother today, what a survivor. Dad's negative attitude toward her never slowed her down. Early on, she wasn't "educated," as people say. Her strong intellect fueled her hunger for learning; she was intelligent and kind-hearted.

Her "can-do" attitude carried her far as she cared and provided for us. Of course, she was a mom and a nurse, but she was even more.

Friend. (*She was admired by everyone she knew.*)

Seamstress. (*With needles, thread, and material,*
she created beautiful queen and wedding dresses.)

Counselor. (*I never tired of time with her;*
hours together flew by.
I felt that she could read my mind!

Cook. (*But she would rather*
someone else does the cooking!)

Quilter and a master at crocheting.

Wife.

Fortune teller.

Community servant.
(*From 1960 to 1967, she served alongside*
many Spanish people in G.I. FORM, a
Hondo-based organization headed by
Henry B. Gonzales, President.

Talented dancer and singer. (*She had some moves*
and a wonderful voice.)

Entrepreneur. (*Although she didn't own a business,*
she knew how to raise money. She often made
and sold tamales on the street.)

Gardener. (*Beautiful flowers brought*
her so much joy.)

Treasured mother. (*In all of life, during happy and not-so-happy times alike, she inspired me. How I miss her, now and always.*)

November 11, 2000

Despite my mother's deep love, protection, and care, childhood was scary. Deep inside, I sense that I was abused, but I'm not clear as to when it happened or who was involved. Perhaps I was too young to remember. Nevertheless, I know.

Then, long before I grew up enough, I married Sal. Surprise, surprise, getting married to Sal didn't make life better. The first year was okay, until I got pregnant with my first child. Instantly, reality hit the fan in clumps. All hell broke loose. (*Sal was almost beyond explanation. At the lowest point, he told others that I was a witch. His "witchcraft friends" confirmed who and what they thought I was.*)

When things seemed hopeless and unbearable, I considered the unthinkable: suicide. No one on this entire Earth stepped in to stop me from taking my life. Yet, God did what God does: He saved my life.

After divorcing Sal, Albert came into my life. Marriage soon followed. And things were a little better. Financial issues dogged us constantly and took a toll on every aspect of our relationship. Eventually, divorce happened. And then, eight years later, we remarried. Inside, I felt better about myself than I had in a long time. I was proud of myself. I had weathered tough times again and came out on the other side. Though many people thought otherwise, I knew I wasn't horrible. I loved my husband. I loved my children and grandchildren. And, perhaps most importantly, I didn't hate myself.

As Thanksgiving, Sonny's and Thelma's birthdays, and Christmas approached, true joy reigned in my mind and heart. I was thankful to God, our heavenly Father, for a brighter life. As always, He watched over all of us. And in my heart, I forgave those who harmed me. The rest lay in God's hands.

On the back side of forgiving, I vowed to strive for a happier life and to love everyone who entered my kingdom, "my home." With God's help, I was determined that my children and grandchildren would have lives free of fear. The curse that hung over my childhood was not going to continue. And in that peace, I rejoiced: *"This is the day that the Lord has made; let us rejoice in it. AMEN."* Psalm 118:24.

March 17, 2001

As I sit at my computer, many memories flood my thoughts:

- I remember Katherine's birth. Her dark eyes fixed on us as we held her.
- Jesse was born in New Braunfels, Texas. He was such an alert baby, always watching me and his dad. That day, I videotaped him; he seemed very happy.

- Taylor Nicole Erskine, my granddaughter, had eyes as bright as the sun; she watched me constantly as I walked all over the place.
- I'm less clear about Rey; he was born in Japan with his grandparents.
- Little Bailey wasn't quite as alert as the others at birth; there were some complications when he was born. Over time, he improved. Now, he's into everything in sight!
- I love my grandbabies. Soon, Stephanie will have a baby of her own, a boy. I hope he will be healthy and as strong as his dad.

Yesterday, Annette and Stephen bought our house; tonight, we are celebrating over dinner. Jesse refuses to go, so he is staying with Aya Ko.

Time passes quickly; Katherine is now 10; Jesse Alexander is 8; Taylor is 4; Old Rey is 3, and Bailey is almost 2.

Later. Love Mom (Ayda Lydia Lovato)

April 20, 2001

It's oyster cook-off day on the west side of town. I know Nina and Stephanie are going. Since oysters aren't my favorite, Albert and I opted for Red Lobster. Yummy! One thing we do well together is eat, eat, eat!

Fiesta Time is just around the corner, and I hope to attend this time. I love the celebration, the fun hats and ribbons, the smell of Mexican food, festive music of all kinds, all the excited, loud people, and even the beer! When I was young, Dad always took us to San Antonio from Hondo for the carnival and parade yearly; at least that's what I remember. "Those were the days," as they say. Life was wonderful then.

Viva Mexico! Viva! The land of the brave!

On a more serious note, I *pray for my children's health today and in the future. Thelma, my baby whom I love dearly, is approaching surgery. As a mother, I can't help but worry, even if she doesn't think the best of me right now. Nevertheless, I still love, and deep down, I know she is in God's hands. I'm not perfect; who is? I know I have done my best with all my wonderful children. And with God, who knows His plans for all of us? No one. I only want what's best for those I love.*

June 25, 2001

It's been a while since I wrote my deepest thoughts in this book. (*Someday, I hope it will be in print for all to read. Who knows.*)

My great niece, Brandi Monique Escamilla, married the love of her life today, Saturday, June 25. She looked beautiful, just like a doll! How my mother would have loved being present for this occasion. If Johnnie, her so-called dad, had been there, he would have cried. (*Back in 1965, he and I were schoolmates. Even though he was crippled, he was cute and brilliant. His parents and mine were best friends.*)

Sal was at the wedding. (*I'd be lying if I didn't admit I still feel "something" toward him.*) We didn't say much to each other; what do I say to a man with no soul? Nevertheless, I strive to respect everyone, although it's hard to do so when someone has hurt you so much. (*Sometimes, when you are at your lowest, you just want to kill that person!*) As we talked, I discreetly put him "in his place" when it comes to keeping up with his children. He's like so many other men who seldom, if ever, stay in touch with their kids. It doesn't make any sense to me. How do you block out your flesh and blood? Sadly, it happens over and over. (*Thank goodness, God never turns His back on us.*) I hope that Sal and I can always be friends, if only by respecting each other, as human beings. With God's help, I have forgiven him. But I will never forget his "going out" with Efrain's daughter, my niece. Unbelievable. (*Both of Efrain's girls have always envied my girls and me. Misplaced jealousy ruins lives.*)

Relentlessly, the sun sets and rises. The tides come and recede. Time never stops. As a fifty-one-year-old woman, I've always striven to respect others through thick and thin. Looking back on my past, I can say things weren't too bad. Now, respect has all but vanished in the young and old alike. Lack of respect for one another stokes hurt.

Sadly, I'll never forget all the horrible, disrespectful things I have seen with my own eyes. There's no rhyme or reason to things that happen in life. Believe me, shit happens. And in those moments, a simple, haunting question remains: "What now?"

I indeed asked myself that question when people tried to take my children away. AS LONG AS I LIVE, THAT WILL NEVER HAPPEN. No personal sacrifice to protect them is too great. They are my world. They are my air, my light, the wind that soars through my soul, and the ground on which I stand.

For their protection and well-being, I moved my children away from Hondo. And now that they are older, they can protect themselves from Satan's evil snares. I pray that they always plant good seeds in fertile soil by focusing on our Savior, Jesus Christ. AMEN!

July 15, 2000

Today, in the *San Antonio News,* I found an interesting article about Yolanda Broyles-Gonzales's newly published book, *Lydia's Life in Music.* Mother picked my name from this book title, hoping I would become a guitar-playing vocalist. However, once I grew up and made plans for my career, I chose a career in medicine over a career in music. Eventually, I became a licensed nurse determined to help those in need.

However, I did enjoy music as a pastime. I've enjoyed lots of things and activities in life. My mom sang to me as a child, and I played the piano, so I followed her example and learned to play the piano. Most often, I played the piano alone and for my enjoyment. I loved playing my favorite sacred hymns and songs that praised God. One of my favorite hymns was "He."

> *He who hears my prayers,*
> *And knows my sins, I say,*
> *He who turns the night to day.*
> *He who knows my dreams and what I believe,*
> *He'll always say: I forgive.*
> *He'll always say: I forgive.*

Our family is celebrating Elijah Ramses Ingram, Stephanie and Tony's newly born son. I love that strong name. He was born on July 12, 2001, at St. Luke's Baptist Health Center Hospital. He weighed 7 pounds 10 ounces and was 21.5 inches long. He is beautiful. God bless that family.

It's almost midnight, and I must work in the morning. Good night. *Muy buenas noches. ¡Hasta la vista, baby!*

August 15, 2001

I learned a lot at work today. Assessments are being graded and put into the computer system. Despite doing very well, I'm still stressed out. Work. Come home. Go to bed. Although I am excited about pursuing my career, I remember those worry-free days of the past. Those wonderful days were filled with my closest friends, my sister Mary, and Belia, though we weren't close then. Jealousy compromised our closeness. In the big picture, I clung to Mom, while Belia clung to Dad. It wasn't until after Belia and I both entered the medical field that we became so close, not even malicious rumors kept us apart. In many ways, we were each other's lifelines, encouragers, and constant sources of support. I couldn't live without her, and she felt the same. Then, for reasons I cannot explain, Satan took the reins in her life, and our relationship suffered. Still, I pray for the Lord to touch her heart and soul.

I'm worried about my dear husband, Albert. PSA levels have risen drastically, which could lead to prostate cancer. He's such a wonderful dad to my children; they're devoted to him. Oddly, I get treated "differently" when he and I aren't living together. Why?

All I can do is leave it in God's hands. Jessie just arrived; he wants to play the piano for me. Later!

October 30, 2001

I have just accepted a new job that will involve extensive travel. Given all that's happening worldwide, my kids are more concerned about my flying. The threat of terrorism looms over us all.

I'm feeling a little conflicted about my kids' feelings toward me. Sometimes, they act like I haven't done enough for them, which is not true; I've given and given to them. Love and peace toward each other are far more important than things and money. Loving one another far outweighs other "stuff." (*I try to remember this with my ex-in-laws, and I respect them and pray they will understand everything that has happened.*)

When all is said and done, I pray my children won't fight over "things" left behind. Most of them are fully grown and incredibly blessed. Besides, Dad and Nina will receive most of the stuff. Above all, I pray that they know I love them beyond words, and that they feel and show love for me.

Kids, remember I created you and know you deeply. Everything will be fine. Live your life with God at the helm. Shun fear and embrace joy. Take care of my grandchildren; always assure them of your constant love, even when they mess up. They NEED YOU, just like you needed me.

Always in each other's hearts.
Your loving mom, Ayda Lydia Escamilla Lovato

January 6, 2002

2001 was quite a year. The world was shaken by terrorism, and I was devastated by my sister Belia hating me. I'll never forget the day Belia, my other sister Juliet Morales, and I were having lunch together. Just as we started to bless the meal, Belia started screaming at me: "Don't touch me, you backstabber!" Neither Tillie, Juliett, nor I had words to explain Belia's outburst. She seemed to be possessed by a demon. The expression on her face and her vicious tone were intensely horrible. Shame and humiliation blanketed me so much that I got up from my seat at the table and ran out. Immediately, Tillie followed me to my car. Tear after tear flowed from my eyes. Peace between us was all but impossible. Regardless, I forgive her for every spoken hateful word and action toward me. I hardly recognized her as my sister; she was different.

The hate that drove terrorists' actions against America on September 11 in New York City flooded into our own lives. America changed forever, and so did my family. How can this world continue when we can't even love those closest to us? We must change; we must forget and forgive. Love must reign in our lives.

Recently, I was going through some of my mother's papers and letters. One of the letters was addressed to my great-grandfather, who had three sons, Refugio, Cristino, and Luciano. I've read the name "Refugio" on Telenovelas on Channel 41. It could be one of our relatives in Mexico City, Mexico. The Escamilla family, close and distant, is scattered all over the United States and Mexico.

As I have shared, I had another grandchild named Hanna Saki Leyva. Like Salvador Leyva, Sr., she has oriental eyes and indescribable beauty.

Albert has a grandchild from his first marriage. If I recall, her name is Ann Marrissa Sanchez. Her mother, Tina Lovato, gave birth in Del Rio, Texas. Her father, Ruben Sanchez, was a police officer in the United States Military Forces.

Later, Tina married and had a beautiful baby daughter. As always, I prayed that her life would be filled with joy.

Albert and I just celebrated our 23rd wedding anniversary. We went downtown to celebrate New Year's, but it was so cold we had to return home. Burr! My heart was warm, but my feet were frozen!

Peace and love to all.

CHAPTER THREE: *2002-2007*

February 8, 2002

Today was a very enjoyable workday at WellMed, a healthcare facility dedicated to delivering the best care to those in need. I guess that's why I keep returning to work, well, that and the income! Helping people has always been one of my highest priorities. (*How I wish my children would work there; it would be a good opportunity for them. And I'd be so proud.*)

My cousin Pedro Escamilla Garza died this week. Tomorrow marks one week since his death. I chose not to attend the funeral since I saw him in the hospital right before he died. Thank God he's now with his mom, dad, and my beloved parents in heaven. Pedro was especially close to my daddy.

Until last year, when a deadly tornado ravaged the city, Pedro was a longtime resident of Hondo. The chaos and physical devastation caused by the tornado took a psychological and emotional toll on Pedro. In my mind, he went downhill quickly after surviving the tornado. Perhaps to put the tornado's impact behind him, he relocated to D'Hanis, Texas. Pedro is survived by his son Pete, who is now married and living in Converse, Texas. In life or death, life goes on. For sure, I'll never forget him.

My son, Salvador Jr., and his Japanese wife, Aya Ko, celebrated the birth of a beautiful baby girl whom they named Hannah Saki Leyva. She weighed slightly over 4 pounds and is healthy. I couldn't be prouder of my son and daughter-in-law. Aya Ko is refreshingly honest, a trait hard to find. I love being close to her.

I think I've already mentioned it, but Tina Marie Lovato Sanchez also had a beautiful baby on December 21st, 2001, just in time for Christmas.

Thanks be to God for all His blessings. I'm so happy to be alive with my children and grandchildren. 'Til next time, chow!

February 26, 2002

Today, I finally got rid of my 1999 Blazer, which has been a complete nightmare. I replaced it with a brand new 2002 Chevy Silverado truck. I am no longer trapped in an embarrassing, useless vehicle. The Silverado is sporty, comfortable, and built for safety. I've nicknamed it Palomino because it feels like I'm perched on a majestic, powerful horse that loves hauling it down the road! (*I even think Dad, Albert, likes it.*)

Recently, Nina moved again, this time with her friend Christi. Without her and Molly the cat, the silence in the house is deafening. They will be missed. I pray that they and Molly will be happy and safe. Honestly, Nina and Christi are almost like sisters; I believe they will take care of each other. To say that I love Nina deeply is an understatement. Her absence brings tears to my eyes. I pray that we never lose our mother-daughter bond.

Just received a call from Esmie. We're planning a candle party on March 16, 2002. I couldn't be happier that she's getting close again. Her laughter and good sense of humor lift me.

It's getting late—almost 10 p.m. Tomorrow is an early day, so I've got to get some sleep. I'm closing for today.

March 29, 2002

Holy Saturday (the last day of Holy Week) has been another excellent day. Of course, we'll attend Easter mass tomorrow at St. John Neumann Catholic Church with Monsignor Bob Silverman. After church, we'll head to Annette's and Stephen's house, 1006 Cibolo Trail, in Universal City, Texas.

Over the years, I've explored and considered being part of various religions and denominations, but I always find my way back to the Catholic Church. I have faith in everything about that Church, plus tons of wonderful memories as a Catholic, especially my wedding day, August 5, 1967. That day, at seventeen, I married Salvador Dominguez Leyva in Hondo, Texas. (*Albert is Catholic through and through, which I like. It's funny how he looks like such an angel at church. But when we get home, it's a different story!*)

Our family is growing so quickly; I already have eight grandchildren. Soon, I won't remember all their names or faces. Mom went through that near the end of her life, and I imagine I will deal with the same.

Sadly, my kids have differing opinions of what it means to be loving, understanding, and friendly with each other. Once they get mad at each other over even the most minor things, they tend to stay angry or upset for a long time. I wish they understood that doing so hurts everyone in lots of ways. I don't know how they are "happy" to stay mad and continue their lives as if the other person doesn't matter.

Holding onto grudges is such a waste of time; it's for the birds! Life happens. Regardless, I choose to be happy, cheerful, and full of life; it's who I am. I love having fun, even if my children don't attend our festivals.

(*Unfortunately, most people must live a while before realizing life is short.*)

Be happy!
Praise the Lord!
Tomorrow, our Lord will rise and shine gloriously forever!
I pray everyone goes to church!
Amen, Amen!

April 10, 2002

I'm proud to claim Hondo, Texas, as my hometown, "Land of the Frogs!" I lived there for thirty years. Recently, Hondo has been hit with severe weather, including destructive tornadoes. I don't remember it ever being so bad when I lived there. I wish I could return, sit under the trees, and think about all the good times. Just the thought of being there makes me feel the gentle breezes and smell the fragrant flowers planted by my mom. Also, we enjoyed eating the peaches, dates, and pecans she picked for us.

Mom was so resourceful, and I was her faithful helper. We'd gather and sell tons of pecans in town; often, she'd earn two or three hundred dollars every time. These dollars helped my sister Belia get everything she needed to graduate.

Home was cherished, even if the house wasn't visually impressive. Yet, it kept us warm during the colder seasons, and we learned to deal with the Texas heat, even without air conditioning! So as kids, we spent lots of time outside. Once we were teenagers, we would often watch people as they walked or drove by. I confess, I enjoyed the looks and winks from guys driving by. (*Any young girl surely enjoyed such harmless attention!*) How silly I was during those teenage years. Haha!

Wonderful memories were formed during those younger years at home. Later in life, after we became adults, nothing was ever the same. After our parents died, I gave half of my parents' property to my sister Belia, which I later regretted. Never could I have imagined that she would become so self-absorbed and selfish. Unfortunately, families aren't immune to bad situations. Life happens. And sometimes, even the good memories evolve into "only memories." What a shame.

May 29, 2002

As of today, I am officially a proud military wife. I've always wanted to be one. But I never imagined it would happen. Albert has been called to active service in the United States Army as part of Operation Enduring Freedom (OEF)—part of our country's response to the September 11 terrorist attacks in New York City. He will be in Afghanistan for a solid year.

I've just returned from visiting with Monseigneur Robert (Bob) Silverman at the St. John Neumann Church. Father Bob has always been there for me; I truly appreciate him.

Unexpectedly, many logistical and legal papers must be processed before Albert leaves. At times, we both feel pressured to get everything done before Albert ships out this coming Friday, May 31, 2002, with his Tough Ombres Unit 238. I am excited and concerned as his wife, yet I know that all the heavenly angels will watch over us and my children. I can't forget to care for them during this time, too. Naturally, we're very emotional about this development.

Albert's a tough man. I believe he will survive this challenge, even with his weak heart. I love him deeply and will miss him greatly. Nights will be lonely and silent. Days will be busy with work and continued education. And in the cracks, I'll take care of all the bills. I hope to pay off everything, which should make him very happy.

While we are separated, we'll both pursue success in our own ways. First and foremost, one must be honest about what is being faced. Albert must survive waging war on behalf of the United States Army, and I must achieve as much as possible on the home front to make our lives even better. All in all, I've been blessed. I pray my children will follow in my footsteps as they grow and mature. I'm not perfect, but I've accomplished a great deal in life.

That's all for now. I'm sure I'll write more once Albert is gone. Writing has always been good therapy for my mind and soul.

June 16, 2002
Unedited email from Dr. Salcher and Marlene,
his wife, while in the jungles of Ecuador

Hi Ayda,

Val and I are sitting here together and decided to try to send you an email. He sent you one and hadn't gotten a reply, so we weren't sure you got it. Don't send any email to that other address if you got it. Send it to this address, and we will probably check them daily and will be waiting to hear from you and the people at the office.

We arrived here on Monday via a six-seat Cessna after flying into Quito Sunday evening. It was a beautiful flight over the

Andes Mountains, and it took only 45 minutes. One mountain was so beautiful because it was covered with snow. One other day this week, we were called to look out at the smoking volcano. Val saw it, but I did not. Later, when I came out of the house, I noticed a snow-capped mountain that I had not noticed a day or two before.

It rains almost every day, and tonight it is pretty cool. There are some beautiful sunny days, and the mountains around here are beautiful.

Hospital work has been pretty light so far, and Carmen is doing a good job translating. I, Marlene, told one of the doctors here about the fact that you could have come, and he said maybe some other time. I think you would have loved the experience.

How is your husband doing? And how are you doing since he left? We are hoping that upon our return, you will come to church with us. Val asks how the people are doing at Greenway? Do we have any news that we need to be aware of?

Well, I guess we will close for now. Val says it's late. How funny, to me, one o'clock in the morning is late. We send our love and prayers to all and tell Teresa, Sharon, and Craig hello for us. God bless you, Ayda.

Val and Marlene

June 30, 2002

It's raining today. Normally, that would make me a bit sad, but not today. Albert's home: he was given some brief leave time away from Fort Hood, Texas. He won't be here long; he ships out to Uzbekistan next Wednesday. Having him at home, even for a few days, makes me happy, and the children don't take as much advantage of me when he is here.

Stephanie is here today. She filed for divorce from Tony Ray Ingram. God knows, she's had plenty of problems. Hopefully, she'll find a job soon and get on with her life. I pray things will be better for her.

Surprise, surprise: Salvador Jr. is upset with me, again. Ayko called last night. She was distraught and complained that Salvador wasn't home. My best advice was for her to get out of the house and go riding. I knew Salvador would get angry at me for butting in, but that's just the way it is. He must grow up fast, get home, and comfort his wife!

All I can do is suggest things that would help them be happier. For some reason, all the kids think life should be easy; well, it isn't. Albert and I pray for their happiness. As parents, it's hard to sit back and let them make their own mistakes. Sometimes, we wondered, "What were they thinking?" As with most young adults, they have minds of their own. They know best, which often leads them to step all over me. Nevertheless, I forgive and move on.

I love all my children dearly; they are so handsome and beautiful, even if I do say so!

Last night, I had a dream about my father. I wondered what he was trying to tell me; usually, it's not good news. I don't remember when he shared good news through my dreams. Hopefully, no one in my family is ill and close to death. But who knows? Life is short.

I'm closing for today; tomorrow's another chance to do life well. As a mom, I hope my children can read my thoughts in the diary. Maybe then, they'll understand all I did or tried to do for their good.

July 21, 2002

Today, the Escamilla family is deeply saddened by the news of my brother, Johnnie Escamilla's, admission to University Hospital. Johnnie, my beloved brother, has a 4-centimeter aneurysm at the aorta. (*Aneurysms are abnormal blood-filled swellings of an artery or vein. The aorta is the main artery from which blood flows from the heart to the rest of the body.*) Johnnie's condition is critical. In my spirit, I do not believe he will survive. Naturally, I want to be at the hospital, but sitting there for hours is useless. I'll sit here and pray for my adored brother.

Johnnie reminds me of my dad; their laughs and ways of talking were almost identical. Once Dad died, Johnnie called me "*mi hija*," which means "my daughter" in Spanish. Often, when he called me on the phone, his first words were:

"Hello! This is your Papa!" (*Of course, later he would say: "Just joking! It's your bro."*) Johnnie frequently gave me sound life advice. And I'll never forget him giving me away the day I married Salvador D. Leyva.

Later tonight, my sisters and I will get together. Hopefully, we will kindly communicate with each other. (*We all resemble each other, including my brothers. Yet, the similarities end there; we are all so very different from each other.*)

Tonight will be challenging and painful. May my brother rest comfortably and sleep well. I'm not sure I have any tears left. Life; if it's not one thing, it's another. Chow for now. Someone's at the front door.

September 21, 2002

Today is a beautiful sunny day.

Albert is still overseas and has just had surgery in Germany. He says he is doing fine and is on his way to Uzbekistan. If I were a magician, I'd make him appear here with me. I just mailed him some pictures; one was of the new 2002 red VW Beetle I bought for him.

While he's gone, I frequently daydream about when we first met. In late July 1978, I worked at my Lydia's Apparel store in Hondo, Texas. One hot afternoon, Albert entered the store searching for new jeans. The jeans he bought that day were slightly too long; he wasn't tall. Trying to be helpful, I told him I would hem them for $2.00. He agreed and later said he just wanted to know if I could sew.

Not long after, Albert began visiting my house in Hondo. Strangely, we talked very little and never kissed. Finally, I asked him: "What do you want?" Without hesitation, he said: "A wife!"

I couldn't believe my ears. After all, I had only been divorced for a week. Albert assured me he wasn't concerned about how long I'd been divorced. As we spent more time together, I observed that he was so kind to the children, which made me happy.

Three months later, I asked: "When do you want to get married?" After a long silence, I said: "Fine. We'll get married during the holidays."

Shortly after Thanksgiving, Albert came home with a huge, 9-foot-tall Christmas tree! (*I was shocked; Sal always took forever to get us a tree.*) The kids were overjoyed and jumped up and down. After we had decorated the tree, I blurted out a huge announcement: "This man is going to be my next husband!" (Oddly, at the time, I was already dating Thomas Cardwell, a white Hondo police officer. Originally from Llano, Texas, Thomas served as a United States Air Force paramedic (PM) and was scheduled for discharge soon. (*On the spot, I quickly concluded that Thomas probably wouldn't be as good with my children as Albert. As the French say: "C'est la vie! – Such is life!"*)

Albert and I were married at the Bexar County Courthouse on January 2, 1979. That day, my sister Belia and I drove ourselves to the courthouse. The whole affair was ... interesting. Albert hadn't even brought money to pay the judge! So, we left and ate lunch at Luby's across from the Plaza and the Courthouse. Luckily for us, we were able to get some cash from one of the newly installed ATMs (automatic teller machines).

With cash in hand, we returned to the courthouse and paid the judge. Humorously, the judge looked at Albert and teased: "Are you sure you want to get married? This whole situation may be a sign that you shouldn't!" We all laughed! And Albert answered shyly: "Yes! I want to marry her!" (*Of course, "her" was ME!*)

That was twenty-four years ago, and now, I sit alone in our lovely home while Albert serves our country overseas. The silence is deafening. The kids are all grown, gone, and busy raising their own. Time is flying by; it seems like I'm getting older fast!

Marrying Albert was the right decision. Who knows what I would have become without him in my life? Albert: my husband, my hero, and so much more. I love him deeply. May God bless him always.

January 3, 2003

Today, I'll spend the day with "all my girls," including my daughters and Ayako, my daughter-in-law. I hope to talk to them about why and how Albert and I returned to each other after John's departure. (*The whole divorced and remarried situation isn't a big secret; we haven't tried to hide anything. Some people know parts or all the details, others don't. All that matters is Albert and me. Nevertheless, I'd like the girls to understand everything.*)

2004 will mark Albert's and my 25th wedding anniversary. I distinctly remember how we got back together after John left. Once John's and my divorce was official, I picked up the phone and called Albert; I wanted him to know John was gone ... forever. Without hesitation, Albert said he wanted to be with me. Finally, after all we'd been through, we both realized that we shared a deep love. We decided that rather than Albert moving, we'd move in his place for Nina and Stephanie's sake. From that moment forward, we decided to follow the Bible's guideline of taking life one day at a time.

Neither of us had imagined that Albert would be called to full-time service in the United States Army, starting May 20, 2002. As that day approached, I became more convinced that this was one of the reasons we were back together: to love and support each other during this difficult time. In the past, regardless of whether we were married or divorced, we always handled our legal affairs. Even if Albert were gone for a couple of weeks, the Power of Attorney would be transferred to me, and we'd do the same this time. But things were different now; our separation would be much longer. I was scared I might never see my husband and best friend again. Every day, we prayed that God would protect Albert while in harm's way and return him safely.

I knew full well that Albert took seriously his call to fight and that he, and every man in the Tough Ombres, 28th Division of the United States Army Reserve, would do whatever was necessary for their country. Kill or be killed by the enemy has always been the harsh reality of war.

Every day Albert was overseas, I prayed, through endless tears, that God would keep him safe. Nothing or no one would keep me from standing by him in good faith as never before. Doing so 'til eternity was my reason for living. As fate would have it, Albert was injured in Uzbekistan. Thank God, his injuries weren't fatal; surgery was necessary. I don't know how I would have lived without Albert, my friend, lover, spiritual companion, and yes, my husband forever.

Albert, I love you very much.
Ayda

March 1, 2003

I'm unsure what to share, but reminiscing about old memories should suffice! My children are always on my mind; they are my best creation. As I've said before, they are all so different. My son, the quiet one, is so intelligent. (*Naturally, the girls may think differently!*)

The girls are a lot like me: loud, peppy, energetic, and always willing to speak my mind freely. While they differ, being with them is always a joy. I miss all of them greatly, and at times, I wish I could turn back the clock to when they were younger.

Currently, I have eight wonderful grandchildren, including Katherine Marie Correa, Jesse Alexander Cortez, Rey Leyva, Hanna Saki Leyva, Taylor Nicole Erskine, Bailey Scott Erskine, Elijah Ramses Ingram, and my step-grandchild, Anamarissa Sanchez. I figure I'll always have plenty of kids around. I hope and pray they will love me as I love them.

That's it for now.
Ayda Lovato

May 18, 2003

I hardly know where to start; so much has happened. Here goes.

Yesterday was Tina's birthday. Albert and I tried to call her military service husband, Ruben, who is stationed in Aviano, Italy. We were unsuccessful.

Although the Germany-based hospital physicians said Albert's injury surgery was successful, he's still in a great deal of pain, and his inguinal hernia was not repaired. That was seven months ago!

My daughter Stephanie has injured her back and has no idea where to turn. No job, money, or husband to care for her.

My family never calls, so I combat loneliness by staying busy with household tasks alongside Albert; that helps some.

Everything has taken a lot out of me.

I often struggle to stay ahead in life. The family is growing, and the grandchildren are getting older so fast. Sometimes I feel so small and insignificant. Yet, I know I can survive it all with God on my side; that's all I need.

I love my family, but the responsibility is enormous. It seems like one of them is at my house every day looking for help with their problems. Probably against all hope, I keep praying they will get closer to God and attend church regularly; it's a slim chance, but I pray. As for me, prayer and being in the Church keep me moving.

Thankfully, I still love my job at WellMed Clinic. The clinic is a bustling family clinic environment, which can make people irritable. Yet, everyone who works there seems to get along well.

Albert and I are still organizing our 25th anniversary celebration for this coming January. The whole event is costly, so I opened a specific bank account into which the kids can deposit money to help with expenses. They are supposed to help, but they seem reluctant to do so. Have they donated money? No, no, no, but no! Whatever; it's all okay; I don't intend to stop helping them. Sometimes they are so selfish and unfair. And I suspect that they talk about me behind my back. How quickly they've forgotten the Ten

Commandments, particularly the "honor father and mother" part. It's all so hurtful that I don't plan on leaving them anything when I die.

God bless my children, for they do not know better.

July 13, 2003

Sometimes, being alone gives one time to focus on the things that truly matter, like: LIFE IS PRECIOUS. Sure, we all have ups and downs, and problems of every variety. And, as always, Satan always hovers by, waiting to take advantage of our every weakness. All he wants is to destroy everything before our eyes.

Now and then, I'm plagued by flashbacks associated with times when things were beyond bad.

Losing my dad was heartbreaking. I felt as if the whole world was caving in on me.

Then, I lost Salvador Dominguez Leyva, the husband/father I thought would take care of me and my children forever. Wrong. What a colossal mistake I made. While on his deathbed, Dad tried to tell me that he was a bad seed. Of course, as always, I thought I knew better. At that time, I was too stupid to listen. I almost feel as if that one bad choice on my part saddled my children's future with a destructive curse. I pray that my children have the power to break that curse throughout their lives.

My second divorce was beyond sadness. Albert and I had everything: each other, wonderful children, and more. How could I have been so stupid, again? Although I felt close to God and the Church, my prayer life was weak and void of spiritual power.

Then, there's my ex-father-in-law, Bentura Leyva. Sadly, I couldn't save him from choking on a piece of meat! I still remember his eyes, tears cascading from his cheeks, and the dark purple facial discoloration right before he breathed his last. Unbelievable. He loved me so much; losing him was devastating. To this day, I always cry when I think of those final moments with him. May he rest in peace.

Next, I lost my dear mother, Maria Isabel Muniz Escamilla. Her final moments on this Earth were so painfully sad. The last time we talked, she clarified that she wasn't ready to leave this world. In her mind, she believed that my sister Belia was trying to kill her, and that's why Belia wanted to take her to Austin, away from San Antonio. Was her fear rooted in truth, or was it an imagined fabrication? Who knows? It all remains a mystery. May God grant her rest and peace.

Jesse Edward Cortez, Annette's violent husband, beat her many times. This last attack on her was terrible, so much so that I had to travel to their small West Texas town to care for Annette, who was seven months pregnant with her future son, Little Jesse Alexander. I burst into tears when I first saw what Jesse had done to her. She was swollen and bruised from head to toe. Her condition was so critical that the police refused to let me take her out of the hospital for trusted treatment from Dr. Carlos Campos in New Braunfels. So, Annette remained in the hospital four more days as medical personnel treated her head fracture and numerous contusions.

My third divorce, from John Albert Bermea, wasn't too nasty compared to other separations. I was eager to return to Albert Lovato and my family; fortunately, the hurried divorce proceedings were designed to allow me to return quickly to my real family.

For a while, things were calm, right up until Stephanie's "loving husband," Tony Ray Ingram, beat her up badly. I have no idea what she is going to do. Similar first-hand experiences give me insight into her entire situation. But, as always, I doubt I'll be allowed to help, now or after I'm gone from this world. I pray that God will protect her before it's too late.

Many painful memories are hidden in my mind and heart. Above all, I'm most concerned about my children. God, help them grow up and take life seriously.

March 2, 2004

Wow, it's been a while. Need to write here! This past year has been crammed full.

Albert is still struggling with depression, unable to work, and just feeling lousy all around. January 9, just a few days after we celebrated our 25th anniversary on the 3rd, Albert fell from our attic and fractured his right shoulder and left wrist. Sometimes it's hard to believe everything that has our way. Thank goodness, all our children, except my son, attended. (*I guess the Lord knew what was coming six days later.*) Salvador Jr. is close to his dad, who may have suggested he not attend the anniversary party. I must say that I will never forget this, as long as I live. Salvador Jr. is so self-centered; everything must go his way or the highway! Until this changes, he'll always suffer.

As I've said many times, the girls seem to have inherited my light-hearted spirit and love of dancing! Even though my dear husband never said so, we all enjoyed dancing at the anniversary party. Albert and I were so delighted that his daughter Tina Lovato Sanchez and husband Ruben were there with their lovely daughter, Anamarissa, in tow. Everyone had a lovely time.

Thankfully, Albert's health is slowly improving. I couldn't be happier. I believe God brought us back together so I could care for Albert. I love him so much; he has been ill for quite some time. (*Albert stayed in some filthy areas in Uzbekistan and Afghanistan. The doctors agree that those unclean conditions contributed to Albert's post-surgery sickness. Unfortunately, Albert never fully recovered from his surgery on September 29, 2002, in Germany.*)

It's time to stop writing for today. Albert's getting hungry, so I'll turn my attention to fixing a salad. For now, bye!

June 12, 2004

This year continues to be hectic and worrisome. Albert had another surgery yesterday; he seems to be doing better. Thelma was the only hospital visitor. I'm disappointed in our children, who seem to lack the time or genuine concern for our well-being. Albert has always been there for them. Maybe it's me they wish to avoid. I'm baffled. (*In my most desperate moments, I wonder whether they will take care of us as we age or just let us die without kind care and love. Who knows how long we'll be here; the Lord says that we should be ready for his return at any time.*)

Albert's erratic health situation worries me day and night. Sometimes his condition is better, then sometimes it's worse. He looks preoccupied and worried, periodically confused and forgetful, and sometimes he seems distant, as if he has lost his mind. (*War takes a toll on a man's mind, heart, and spirit.*) I wish God would heal him. He means everything to me—my heart would break if I lost him.

I'm sure my children will continue with their lives after I'm gone and survive in whatever way they can. May God's angels watch over and protect them, for they know little about life and death.

I've always been curious as to why I was brought up in the Baptist church; now and always, despite periods of religious confusion, I am committed to Catholicism. Dad's church attendance fluctuated. I don't recall going to church with him until I was fifteen. Before that, who knows where he was on Sundays? He always claimed to be in church on Sundays, and I believed him. Albert's dad attended the Catholic Church faithfully and encouraged us to do the same. (*Fortunately, both dads were on the same page about the Catholic Church. Today, the Roman Catholic Church is where I belong, and I pray that my children will return to it.*)

I turn to the Bible for guidance, especially when I'm alone. Mom's favorite Bible passage is Psalm 91. It speaks to me as well, but I particularly enjoy the book of Proverbs. (*It has thirty-one chapters, one for each day of the month*)

When I feel concerned or threatened by Satan, I usually turn to Ephesians 6:11:

"Put on the whole armour
of God, that ye may be able
to stand against the wiles of the devil."

In closing, my loving advice to my kids and everyone else is to read the Bible now and then.

March 25, 2005

This morning, I woke up thinking about my recent trip to Hawaii; its magical breezes and gorgeous vistas still linger in my mind. Thelma Lynn and Joseph Erskine, along with their family, were so generous and friendly to my daughter, Annette, and me. Every day was filled with fun, but I missed my family. I've returned to work at WellMed, Greenwood Park, but I'm still "floating on air" from the trip.

Since returning, I've visited several people. Today, I saw my sister, Tillie, and finally touched my sister, Belia E. Aguilar. Seeing her look so well and in good spirits was amazing; she seemed like the sister I remember.

Dad (Albert) and I are well; he is attending school, and I'm working hard as usual. On the other hand, my brother Johnnie Escamilla isn't doing so well. Despite having a bad liver, he often drinks straight liquor.

On a happier note, this weekend we celebrate Easter, commemorating the day Jesus rose from the grave after being crucified. Amen.

After Easter, we plan a trip to Gering, Nebraska, where Albert will attend his 25th high school reunion. I hope Albert's health doesn't keep him from going; he's complaining about pain in his left groin area. This will probably be the last time we travel that far by car. My vision is waning, and I can't drive there without help. (*Nina and Sid Rangel plan to travel with us again; they enjoyed the last reunion. The only sad thing about going will be seeing Mom and Dad Lovato's home, but they won't be there.*)

Lately, depression has kept me from writing often in my journal. But today, I feel great.

As I close, I find myself focusing on and worrying about Stephanie. She seldom sleeps and often wanders around like a crazy fool. I always pray for her and Elijah; may God bless them.

May 15, 2005

As usual, numerous activities are taking place. Annette and I attended a Spurs basketball game as part of our Mother's Day celebrations. We had VIP tickets! The outing was such fun.

Yesterday, I met Stephanie's boyfriend, Michael Bradshaw; hopefully, she's found her Prince Charming. Stephanie means the world to me.

Since last year, I've been dealing with diabetes. Fortunately, I've been able to manage it through dietary adjustments. My son also deals with diabetes; I pray he can control it without prescription medications. Annette and Stephanie also have diabetes; I guess it runs in the family genes. Thelma and Nina remain disease-free. If they watch their weight closely, all should be fine.

This year, we celebrated Albert's 57th birthday. The event was terrific. Albert's health remains a mix of good and bad. He still complains about issues with his left groin. Next month, he has a routine follow-up with his surgeon, who plans to explore the area with a scope to determine the cause of the issue. Of course, as needed, surgery will follow.

We also hope to visit Ernest (Ernie) Lovato in Albuquerque, New Mexico, and Albert's uncle, who lives in an assisted living facility. We'll connect with Lloyd Lovato in Phoenix, New Mexico; we may take him to Albuquerque.

September 17, 2005

Today has been quiet and peaceful; I love days like these. Annette spent last night here; she's still recovering from surgery two weeks ago. Little Jesse and she argued quite a bit. He's far too old not to know better. He seems to enjoy irritating his mother. I do not know where their mother/son relationship will end. We love them both immensely and pray for them daily. As a grandparent, we don't want our Little Jesse to grow up.

Thelma is still visiting her family in Hawaii. Two more years before she returns home.

Tina Marie is in New Mexico. Finally, she and her family just returned home from Italy.

Despite not feeling himself, Albert started painting a home for a lady in our area. It's over 100 degrees here; I pray he will be okay. While he works, I sit here just wondering about everything. I'm happy and comfortable here with Albert. The children seem well; I sure hope it stays that way.

All I can do is pray, always! That's one lesson I've learned in life.

I'll share this with all my family and friends: pray and attend the Roman Catholic Church.

October 6, 2005

When I wake up, I think of God,
I pray, and think what it would be,
Without my job so near, you see.

I'm glad I work for WellMed,
It's where I want to be.
It also keeps me "Well-fed ..."
But this is the key.

Not only to keep my patients,
But also, to lead them here,
Where good people attend their needs,
This is where I want to be.

I've been nursing for thirty-six years,
And now that I think back,
WellMed has the lead ...

To increase the health care,
And meet ours and their needs.
Thanks to God and Dr. Rapier,
For I pray he'll always be here.

Ayda L. Lovato, LVN.
WellMed @ Greenway Park

If indeed you are Emmitt, why do you not call me? I don't like communicating via email very much, because anyone can claim to be you.

Email response from Ayda Lovato

Just wanted to tell you, I miss you lots!

Luv,
Demmit (Ayda Lovato)

Handwritten Notation
March 30, 2006 – 18:20

I called Bea; she insisted I meet with her first before visiting. She stated she didn't want to talk and have my family as audience. I agreed to meet soon; she said she would call me.

Ayda Lovato, LVN

August 26, 2006

The weather is beautifully sunny today, and I'm caring for Elijah. Elijah watched cartoons as he and I had breakfast with Grandpa Albert.

Later, we're attending a wedding in Schertz. A member of Albert's Knights of Columbus is getting married. Hopefully, all will go well. Thereafter, I'll go to Liz Bradner's house; she's my sister's daughter.

I'll probably spend the night, allowing me to get out of my children's hair for a while. (*I seem to always be in the way. I feel like I'm a bother. Unwelcome. And any time I state my opinion, they often seem aggravated.*)

Albert and I are fine; there are no significant problems. Tina visited last week; her presence always changes Albert's mood. He probably wants to be left alone with her. I'm pretty sure that's her mother's wish.

I pray that someday Tina will accept me as her stepmom. Despite thinking like her mother, she seems to be nice. (*Like her mom, Tina is frequently negative and tends to sneak around regarding plans connected to her mom.*)

Albert is outside mowing the lawn. He's always followed his Grandpa Lloyd's advice to have a lovely house and yard and be a good husband and person. (*He's a wonderful dad, but at times, like many men, a lousy husband.*)

That's all for now. Next time, I'll focus more on happy moments in my life.

Advice for the Day: Always wake up like you have a thousand dollars in your hand!

September 10, 2006

It's Sunday; lots of news to share.

My grandson Jesse Alexander Leyva Cortez is in juvenile jail. While our family loves him immensely, we are saddened by some of his actions toward others. No one understands what motivates him to misbehave. Sadly, he'll spend his birthday in jail. At times in the past, he's told me that he wishes to be a criminal for the rest of his life. I refuse to believe that.

I don't understand why he chooses to associate with those in the nasty world of drugs and evil behavior. He needs great love and an educational opportunity in a special school. He also needs to be watched carefully for unusual behaviors. With help, he can become the great grandson I know he is!

Truth be known, he has broken my heart many times. Nevertheless, he is the love of my heart, and I will never stop loving him. (*Instead of pointing fingers and being critical, I wish all my children would join forces and help pay for whatever counseling is needed. Jesse's life would improve 100% if we just came together and planned. Sadly, Jesse may only learn "the hard way." But we must not give up; he needs help with his illness.*)

None of us is perfect. We all have flaws. We aren't saints. We can't hide! Jesse hasn't learned that eventually, everything comes out in the open.

I pray I live long enough to see him live a better life in this ridiculous, confusing world.

May God bless my family, now and always.

February 8, 2008

This past year, 2006-2007, has been horrible.

Albert appears to be doing worse, struggling with memory and performing simple tasks. He got an MRI of the brain; the results concluded that he has dementia. Albert's psychiatrist, Dr. Hernandez, prescribed Aricept, but the man refuses to take it.

I try to think positively about life, but it's exhausting when your children are constantly upset, sick, or too busy to come by and make sure everything is okay. Regardless of how they think, I love them. I pray that they will never again doubt my love when they read this.

Nina and Isidro Rangel are getting married in the Catholic Church this year. It has cost me a lot, but she is finally getting closer to the Church. I pray that continues. The wedding will allow me to see all the Escamillas, the Lovatos, and the Rangels, my entire family!

Family can be taxing. My children are doing well for now, but I still struggle to show my love in a way they'll accept. It is difficult to ask for a hug. Often, their eyes scream anger. I dare not ask "What's wrong?"

Recently, Albert and I processed our will. It's designed to protect us from others who want to take away what we've worked for.

Children, learn from my mistakes!

We, your parents, aren't going to be here forever. Every day is borrowed time. Tomorrow is never guaranteed.

Forgive me if I made you feel left out. It was never my intention.

If possible, I'd leave all of you money and houses.

Having "things" in life doesn't breed happiness.

Family is most important. Having a mom and dad ... is priceless!

CHAPTER 4: *2008-2025*

October 18, 2008

It's been quite a while since I've written in my book. Life has been full of problems.

Albert has improved since December 2007, but struggles with depression. There was a time when he didn't take his anxiety medication. So, now, I monitor that he does.

Finally! I saw my daughter, Nina, marry Sid; the whole wedding was a thing of beauty, something I always wanted for all my children. (*All the other weddings weren't exactly what I dreamed; I couldn't attend Salvador's wedding in Japan. I dearly wanted to be there, but it wasn't possible. I cried the entire day.*)

Sadly, I lost another brother this year, Efrain M. Escamilla. On May 20, 2008, I ruptured the L5-S1 disc on the right side of my spine. (As a nurse, I knew this wouldn't be fun. Medical personnel refer to this lower back area as the lumbosacral joint, a transitional point where physical weight loads are transferred from the spine to the pelvis and legs.)

The entire ordeal was emotionally and physically demanding; I thought I was going to die. Honestly, dying would be far better than "living" my final days confined to a nursing home! God knows I'd rather die than be subjected to that. Surely, my children, for whom I have sacrificed so much, would not relegate me to a single room in a horrific adult care facility. (W*hat goes on behind many of those closed doors is appalling.*)

In my mind, I felt like I was ahead of the dying game, having already prepared a last will. As is often the situation, my children and extended family openly disagreed with many details listed in the will, including the stipulation that Tina Marie Sanchez never be allowed to take over my house. (*Albert will find a way to give her something substantial. She won't be left out.*)

Tina was raised by her grandparents. In the process, she was told many lies about me; consequently, she has never trusted me. Nevertheless, I only wished her well. In my heart, I only wanted two things for her: I hoped that she would always love, respect, and appreciate her dad, and – perhaps against all odds – I wanted her to be like a daughter to me. However, surrounding circumstances and lies prevented that from becoming a reality. That's why I refused to put her name on any of my belongings. I'm sure she does not wish to be reminded of me when I'm gone. Besides, Albert will make a way to leave something for her.

Then, there's Jesse, who I truly wanted to have and use my piano! (*I always find it so relaxing to play while at home alone, without anyone around criticizing how you're playing.*)

Furthermore, because my blood runs through my children's and grandchildren's veins forever, I was determined that when I died, they would receive something that would not allow them to forget me. (*No one wants to be forgotten.*)

Honestly, looking back, I've done so much for my kids, including providing them with constant loving care when they were young, and working as many as five jobs simultaneously to meet their physical needs. Additionally, for their sake, I figured out ways to cope with Albert's outrageous behavior and Delia, his ex-wife, who was always intensely jealous of me, to the point where she never wanted Albert and me to see Tina.

I was exhausted and couldn't continue carrying everything on my own. To this day, I don't recall anyone ever saying: "May I help you?" The silence was deafening. Never could I have imagined all the divorce-related outcomes. Surely everyone realizes that couples have ups and downs; it's called marriage! Yet, I felt as if everyone thought I was plain wrong for leaving Albert. (*This wasn't the first time I felt profound loss after a divorce. Stephanie was only one and a half when I left Salvador. She was too young to understand what was happening. Nevertheless, I promised God that I would do everything possible to be both mom and dad to Stephanie. Years later, her displeasure with me surfaced; she made it clear that I had just failed.*)

Throughout the Albert ordeal, it seemed as if everyone, and I mean EVERYONE, criticized me, spat on me, and stomped around in anger and frustration, like infuriated, make-believe cartoon characters with steam shooting out of their ears! The outrage was unbelievable.

And, when all was said and done, I lost a lot, even my children, for a while. Perhaps I hadn't considered what might happen after leaving Albert. Despite all the challenges, God's divine providence – and Father Bob's pastoral care – remained steadfast; I was never forsaken.

In the wake of all this, I decided to make the most of life. Without a doubt, my life has not been easy.

Almost killed by Sal; saved by Albert.
Almost killed – again – by my David; saved by John.
John left me for another woman; saved again by Albert.

Now, Albert and I have made the will.
And, of course, everyone's mad – again.

Some days, I have no idea which way to turn. And, regardless of what direction I take, it will be wrong in someone's eyes.

Now, I'm disabled; soon, I'll never work again. What will happen next? My only prayer is that someone will care for me with a genuine sense of dignity and love.

Final thought: Day ... is a beautiful day. I have my children, my husband, and my grandchildren. Forever love to all!

September 4, 2009

Gosh, things are moving at a snail's pace today at work; I'm bored, again. I only have one more hour in my shift.

Nothing major is going on in the family.

Jesse's seventeenth birthday is approaching; just nine more days to wait. His girlfriend, Samantha Gilbreath, is pregnant with their second child. Hopefully, Jesse will find a job or join the military to support Samantha and the kids.

I'm overjoyed that Annette is happy at this point in her life.

My family is growing so quickly. It's hard to believe I'm a great, great-grandmother. Watching my children become grandparents is truly enjoyable. (*At times like these, I can't help but think of Mom. Sometimes she didn't know what to do.*)

Thankfully, Albert is improving.

Everyone, except me, seems to be doing well. Most of the time, I don't feel too well. On a good note, the back surgery I had a little over a year ago (June 24, 2008) was successful. Thank goodness, I'm doing so much better. (*Oddly, I have a hard time remembering details surrounding the surgery, including the two months, May and June, I had to miss work. Even now, a year later, I still forget things, including work-related matters. It's crazy! Some mornings, I need to remind myself to get up, dress, and go to work. My kids think I'm*

83

"faking" the memory loss, but it's not true. I really can't remember things. Why would I ever fake that?)

Health issues aside, I still love going to work. It's hard to put into words the satisfaction I feel from helping those in need. The expressions on their faces bring me joy. Sometimes I feel like I know better how to help them than their doctors! Nurses spend so much more time with patients than doctors do. Compared to other jobs I've had, WellMed is a breeze! Besides, my deep commitment and involvement with patients help me shift the focus away from personal concerns, such as Albert. God knows, he's such a handful! Like most older folks, he can be very stubborn. Usually, I take a breath and guide him forward. Then, at other times, I leave him alone. Balancing my work responsibilities with taking care of him can be difficult. But I figure out ways to get it all done. (*I try not to focus on what will happen when all of us are unable to take care of ourselves and others.*)

That's it for today.

September 11, 2009

Today is a regular workday, and it's raining outside. The rain seems to be keeping people away, but of course, that could change at any time.

Tomorrow, Annette is having a get-together for Jesse; I hope it goes well.

Albert is remodeling my bathroom. I hope it's done by Jesse's party.

My kids are doing well now.

My brother, Oscar, and my sister, Tillie, are the only siblings who come to my house. (*That's just fine with me!*)

Almost all the time, I take care of Elijah; what a funny little boy, and he's growing up so quickly. I'm happy that he's safe; there was a time when I worried that his dad, Tony, might hurt or kill him.

Jesse and Samantha Gilbreath will soon have their second child; Jesse will need to "up his game" regarding child support.

Stephanie is working so hard as a student at Phoenix College. The non-stop schedule wears her out to the point where she overslept and arrived at work late today. She needs to explore other jobs.

Annette loves her job at The Scooter Store in New Braunfels. I think she works in the claims department.

Nina, who has three cats and three dogs, and no kids on the horizon, works from home in the appeals department at PacifiCare Health Systems; she loves her work.

Sonny is quite happy with his job. He works as a mechanic and tools and parts manager for the US Postal Service.

Thelma runs her home-based business, Lasso by Design. Her company manufactures rosaries, necklaces, and other types of jewelry. Although she enjoys this work, she aspires to work in the medical field, particularly in sonography and different roles that involve working with young women.

That's it for now!

November 19, 2009

Another day at work. Too bad I can't be outside; the weather is beautiful. Albert's home, I think. Just talked to Thelma, who's in Dayton, Ohio. Jesse's in a private school associated with a juvenile detention program, where he's safe from druggies who offer him pot. (*Annette just visited him and reports that he seems calm.*)

As for me, I'm dealing with some pain in my left leg. Some days are worse than others. As necessary, I take 800 mg of Motrin when I can't handle the extreme pain. Although I am disabled, the doctor won't go on the record as saying that I can't continue working. Some days are easier than others. I certainly hope to continue working at WellMed; this December marks ten years since I began there. Exciting!

The only negative aspect of my work is that I often feel bored with the routine. Maybe I'm just preoccupied with family matters. My sister, Juliette, bugs me with her constant talk about various family members. I asked her to stop. I told her I would stay home and mind my business. (*I haven't*

heard from her since! Occasionally, someone–namely me–
needs to stand up for others in our family!)

Enough of this; back to work!

December 21, 2011

Four more days until Christmas ... and I'm at work! (*WHAT AM I DOING HERE?!*) Despite loving my job, all I want at this time of year is to be at home, wrapped in warm clothes, relaxing in front of my fireplace. Just four more hours and I can head home!

As usual, a lot is going on at home; never a dull moment.

Kids get angry for a bit, then make up on their own.

Two grandchildren are coming soon: one from Nina, the other from Stephanie.

Stephanie's custody case is scheduled to go to court soon.

Thelma just had a tummy tuck!

Annette is working part-time at United Parcel Service (UPS) and hopes to advance to full-time status.

Sonny still isn't talking to Albert; that's bad, bad. Most people don't like his mouth, but what can you do? Things are what they are. Sadly, I feel as if I'm losing my brothers, but thankfully, I'm still holding onto my sisters.

It feels good to write down my thoughts again; it's been a while. I'll be back soon. 'Til then, bye! Hope you enjoyed the read!

August 8, 2012

Today, things have been good at work; I'm not so busy that I can't daydream about home stuff. As always, I enjoy my job, but I love to be at home.

Things are calm on the home front. Not too much happening.

Albert got a new car this year, planning to use it on our June 2013 trip to Nebraska. Albert loves going there, but we always must figure out what to do with our dog, Buster. He always seems so forlorn when we leave him.

Soon, Thelma is moving to Tampa, Florida. I pray she will be okay; her brain tumor always concerns me. I worry a lot about her health.

Ruby Olivia got baptized on August 5th; what a joyous day. Nina and Sid were delighted, and both grandmothers beamed.

I'm still grieving over losing Ysabel Selena. (*Talking to her inside her mommy's tummy was precious. I miss that so much. I will always love her.*)

Stephanie seems to be doing better. But honestly, we both struggle with periods of unhappiness.

June 27, 2014

Wow, it's been two years since I've taken time to write in my book. I have been busy!

I married, divorced, and remarried.

Presently, I'm married to Camilo Garza Carranza. We met a long time ago; he was nineteen and I was seventeen. We reconnected at Taylor's, my granddaughter's, 16th birthday, August 2013. Shortly thereafter, Camilo started calling me.

At that time, I was still married to Albert, who wanted to retire; the only problem would be that we'd be home together a lot. That's something I didn't want to do. Few people knew or understood the life I had with Albert. His ways were strange, primarily because of his post-traumatic stress (PTSD) issues.

Nevertheless, I did everything I could to help Albert. Unfairly, he told the Veterans Administration Hospital personnel that I was the reason he was sick. Knowing that he felt that way after fifteen years of marriage was hurtful.

On more than one occasion, we sought marriage counseling; once, he even brought my daughter Nina to the session. To say that I felt embarrassed, shameful, worthless ... or completely void of dignity, was an understatement. Facing

Nina was impossible. Eventually, I lost hope that the marriage could be repaired. So, I gave up and filed for divorce. As soon as I informed Camilo about the situation, he asked me to move in with him. Ten months later, Camilo proposed, and I accepted.

Days, weeks, and months passed, and eventually my joy and confidence about marrying Camilo shifted to uncertainty, anger, and periodic depression. (*Not exactly what I had hoped.*)

Two years later, things improved. I love Camilo deeply for many reasons: he's honest, kind, and it's apparent that he loves me. Without fail, he always kisses me goodnight.

Although I felt better about the marriage, my relationship with my children was beyond rocky. (*Sometimes it seems impossible for everything to be good simultaneously; it's very frustrating.*) Month after month, neither my son nor my daughters spoke to me. (*I believe Albert is the reason my children hate me and seldom, if ever, visit me. We are blanketed by sadness.*)

Despite all, my love remains for my children, grandchildren, great-grandchildren, and great-great-grandchildren. I love them all forever.

August 5, 2014

I'm here, ready to write, but for some reason, I can't get started. Today is my grandson Bailey Scott's sixteenth birthday. As I have said many times, I deeply love my children, grandchildren, and great-grandchildren (Jesse Ryan and Kevin Aurthur Cortez, Zaeden Charles Hale, Elaina Martinez Cortez, Orion Leo Serna, Marina Elzbeth and Leona Erskine).

Almost one year ago (April 2014), my ex-sister-in-law, Virginia Carranza, was hospitalized with advanced-stage cancer and severe congestive heart failure. While she was hospitalized, I agreed to temporarily help Camilo, her husband, with their daughter Jessica.

As days passed, doctors eventually told the family that Virginia's health issues had significantly advanced and that her prognosis was bleak. Her life was nearing an end. Within a few days, Virginia died. Soon after, Camilo asked me to move to Taylor, Texas, to help care for his daughter, Jessica. Naturally, I was eager to be of assistance; family helps family. Consequently, I moved to Taylor on April 14, 2014.

Once in Taylor, I did all I could to encourage Camilo as he began his complex grief process. Additionally, I helped him process all the other logistics associated with losing a spouse. Together, we cleaned and purged his home of Virginia's no longer needed belongings. It was painful for us both. Through tears, we pulled out Virginia's clothes from all the closets and took them to the local Goodwill Industries Donation Center.

Although I primarily moved to Taylor to help Camilo and Jessica, I found myself praying that the move would be more than that. Inside, I was desperate to find real peace, love, kindness, and whenever possible, some much-needed relaxation.

As expected, moving to a new place was difficult on many levels, including missing my family. However, that family longing was offset by not feeling under constant stress, unlike at home with Albert. (*Dear God! Only He knows what I have gone through with Albert. How I wish my children knew how difficult it was to handle and care for Albert.*)

Like so many other times in my life, it seemed as if I couldn't win for losing. Seldom has anyone understood my life decisions. Now, neither my husband, Albert, nor my children comprehended the details of my situation. Albert just wouldn't let me go. I think he refused to do so because I was making good money, which provided financial stability as he dealt with his issues. And, as always, I had done everything in my power to care for my children. It seemed my best wasn't enough for my children, nor Albert. (*In my lowest moments, I believed that he never really loved me.*)

All things considered, it's not surprising that I went through periodic depression. I missed my kids. I hated fighting in court with Nina and Stephanie. I'd be lying if I said that I never thought about destroying myself.

Camilo and Tillie carried me through some of the worst times. Now, finally, I believe I have overcome much of the negativity. I am retired from nursing, and I feel like I have regained my sanity. Now and then, I smile! I've taken a new direction for the better, and I'm walking more freely day by day.

I have learned to love Camilo despite his advanced age and difficult sickness. He is a wonderful, unselfish man. Our relationship thus far, though intimate and tender, has not included pre-marital sex, just kisses and closeness. I hope that someday we will become husband and wife, for all time.

To my children, I love and miss you greatly.

Annette, I love you.
Sonny (Salvador Jr.), I love you.
Thelma, I love you.
Stephanie, I love you.
And, Nina, certainly not last nor least, I love you.

Besos (kisses) to all!

October 14, 2014

Today started joyously; I ate breakfast at The International House of Pancakes (IHOP) with Tillie. We had so much fun together.

As we ate, I explained to her that Camilo and I were recently married. As clearly as possible, I tried to explain to her how much we love each other, as well as our mutual desire to care for one another in life, through both the good and the bad.

Looking back, I see more clearly how Camilo often defended me from Salvador. (*Salvador, the so-called father of my first four children.*) In many ways, I feel as if I am returning the favor to Camilo. (*For the record, we never slept together. I guess we were just old-fashioned. So, all the hateful names my children called me, their mother, the woman who brought them into this world, were uncalled for! Blah, blah, blah! And when I decided to retire, good grief. Thelma and Stephanie were so upset about it. It's my life, not theirs. I would never have spoken to my mother that way; never. Sadly, Camilo was also on the receiving side of their disrespect.*)

For obvious reasons, I spend a great deal of time with Camilo's kids and the extended, large family (10 kids!). (*Finally, God gave me the ten children I always wanted. Virginia, my former favorite sister-in-law, would be so proud of me. I can see her looking down from heaven and smiling at me. We always pray for her, even though she's above. May she always walk in and enjoy God's eternal peace.*)

In my heart, I realize that my family is broken. God knows I never meant to hurt them in any way. A mother's love for her children is a deep, vast ocean. No matter what, it never goes away. Life. Love. Education. Hugs. Kisses. I gave them everything precious.

But today, I am delighted to be a member of the Carranza clan. I am happy, comfortable, and confident that Camilo and his family love me, just like I've always been a part of them.

Besos and amore (love and kisses) to all!
Tu Madresita que simper los quera (your mother who always loves you)

March 1, 2015

It's cloudy today, which makes me feel sleepy. Camilo is working on a rosary to sell while he listens to gospel music. That's what we do on Sunday mornings. Except for the hole in my heart from missing my children, everything seems good today.

My children don't understand who their mother is. I am a good person. I don't hate or intentionally hurt others, and I have never killed anyone. I am simply a mom who loves her children. How I wish they would remember how hard I worked to put food on the table, keep them healthy, and more. (*Why do children forget so easily?*) God knows, I love them.

As on many days, I am blanketed in sadness due to not seeing my kids. I need them. They have been ripped from my heart and soul. Without her children, a mom isn't a mom. Why don't they understand that? Now that I'm retired, I have endless time to think about everything. Not knowing whether they are healthy, sleeping well, eating well, or in need of financial help breaks my heart. And most of all, I can't help but wonder if they miss their smart, loving mom. Bottom line: I'm just a mom.

February 25, 2017

This year has been eventful. One significant development is that I'm attending college. So far, I am enjoying the academic challenge and the progress in my life; emotionally, it's a good distraction and a positive step forward.

Life with my husband's kids isn't great like it was early on. Honestly, I cannot stand one of the kids, and I'm weary of dealing with her ridiculous ways, especially her hurtful gossip. (*Her gossipy talk pisses me off and usually leads us to fight. Whatever! As long as she keeps quiet, I'll be fine.*)

God knows, I want to run away and go back home. I'm fine when at school, but otherwise, it's almost more than I can tolerate. And as for Camilo, I try to ignore him most of the time.

Today, I went to eat in Pflugerville; it was a good distraction from so many sad, unfixable things. After I came home, I took a nap. Camilo also lay down for a bit. Afterwards, I decided to visit the telephone company to cancel Jessica from our phone plan. She is constantly on her phone and using up all our gigabytes. Sadly, that wasn't possible until she decided to pay for her way, which I doubt will ever happen. (*Sometimes, I wish she would move far, far away from us.*)

Most of the rest of life is okay. I feel like things are in a good place with the boys. We love each other mutually. And my son wants to visit; how I wish he would. I believe that he and Camilo would get along well. They are both Scorpios! (*Scorpios are known for being passionate, somewhat mysterious when it comes to revealing their feelings, loyalty, and more.*)

That's all for today. I will try to write again soon.

October 11, 2018

Well, so much for finding time to write "soon." It's been over a year since I've had time to write a journal entry. As usual, many things have happened.

Camilo had cardiac surgery on April 4th, followed by heart bypass surgery on September 13th.

Currently, I feel exhausted, yet I've managed to handle everything in life.

Every so often, I find myself wondering about "who wants what" when I die. I so want Taylor to have the piano, but she still isn't talking to me. So, who knows?

I am willing to give Hannah my bedroom furniture; I think she will be responsible and take care of it.

My jewelry goes to Annette. Then, she can share some of it, such as rings and other items, with her sisters as she chooses. (*I think they will all want something from their mother.*)

I want to leave my computers with Jesse. (*Jesse, don't forget to erase everything!*)

The living room furniture can go to Bailey, Elijah, or Rey; whoever wants it.

It may seem morbid to focus on such things, but I know I won't live much longer due to my blood sugar levels. I can't seem to get those levels under control. I guess a few people want to die, but not me. I'd rather live, but "that's life!" There's no guarantee of tomorrow. And if tomorrow comes, who knows what it will bring. We are born to suffer, then die.

As always, I love all my children, grandchildren, and great-grandchildren. (*I so miss Isabel Selena. I look forward to seeing her in heaven.*) Every child means the world to me. And when I think back about how deeply I loved and respected my parents, I shake my head. Never could I have imagined that I would experience such rejection from my children.

When I think about dying, and I don't mean to be negative, I can't help but pray that before I am gone, I at least might understand why Thelma and Stephanie hate me so profoundly. I miss them so much and forever wish them joy in life and forgiveness from God above.

As for me, I cry a lot. Sometimes, the cumulative weight of everything across the years is too much to bear. On the other hand, I love much of my new life. Unlike my ex-husbands, who viewed me as little more than a means to financial security, Camilo loves me deeply. (*As I look back, I seldom got anything but utter disdain and hatred from Salvador and those that followed until Camilo.*)

Life with Camilo has been peaceful, to the point where I love life, albeit a life of agonizing isolation from my children. I keep myself busy in retirement with fun activities like making tamales. Thank goodness I don't need my children to support me. Money isn't a struggle. (*What would happen if I did?*) I also knit, play the piano, and care for Camilo. That's my life. Everything else is beyond my control. I can't fix everything from the past or in the present. My children are grown; what they decide is their own decision.

In closing, may God bless my entire family, and may they come to understand my heart and nature. I'm honest, lovable, friendly, cheerful, playful, and respectful of others. (*How can my children not know this about me? At least people from work loved me. I still have old friends from those days who still want to talk to me. Yet my own family ...*)

May 17, 2021

Loss has again come my way; Camilo, my ever-so-kind, unselfish husband, died on March 3, 2021. Again, I'm alone. Fortunately, he died peacefully, without struggle. Now that he's gone, his kids never talk to me. It's fine; I am good with that.

Healthwise, I'm better than I imagined a while back. Despite not drinking and smoking, I recall thinking that my end was near. Maybe I was just overloaded with hurt and disappointment. Regardless, I am determined to look ahead to a normal, hopefully long, future.

My grown kids seem to be softening toward me. I can hardly express how grateful I am for that change. Sadly, Stephanie is still buried in inaccurate perceptions about me. Every day, I pray that changes. I need my kids, and my love for them is endless.

Recently, I visited Tom Powell in Rockport, right on the Texas coast. Tom's wife, Sharon, who recently passed away, was one of my treasured former coworkers. Tom is a true friend. I also traveled around a bit with my friend Carole Nelms. Those visits were so enjoyable. I'm breathing easier about life. I'm single and a happy camper about how life is right now.

However, I am worried about Annette; Jesse is such an asshole toward her and Stephen. To say that he is "trouble" is an understatement. I fully expect that someday he will be in jail for a very long time. I hate to say it, but that's what he deserves.

Taylor is now living on her own, and that's a good thing.

Except for Nina's kids, almost all my grandchildren are grown up. Nina's little ones are so cute!

Kat needs a home of her own. I pray that God will provide what she desires and needs.

And, as much as I would like to fix everything with my kids, I can't. We all have our problems. I need to take care of myself, and they, as grown men and women, must do the same. For now, I stay at home and keep clear of their business.

Before closing, let me say that I need to relax and be happy at my own home. Peace is my greatest wish and need. Having things otherwise really bothers me and often makes me physically ill.

I can't believe it's been so long since I wrote in my book. I'm ok and safe at home.

October 30, 2021

Today is wonderful! Recently, I met my future husband, Jose A. Acosta. Without a doubt, I know he will be a good provider, but perhaps more importantly, he makes me laugh. I love him to death. We plan to get married soon in Hawaii; I never could have imagined marrying in such a beautiful place. Honestly, I don't know precisely how all this will be in the future, but for now, I AM HAPPY, and not alone in this harsh world.

Jose is a great person. Curiously, I've known his family for nearly three decades. Consequently, I am confident that the wedding will be a joyous occasion for all in attendance. As of now, Stephen and Annette will travel with us to Hawaii for the wedding. We look forward to having a wonderful time. Jose and I couldn't be more thrilled to join our lives. (*How I wish Tillie could attend; she's getting too old for such adventures. But she will be with us in spirit.*)

As expected, some of my kids think I'm crazy; not so! What's crazy about being happy with the man you love? (*I can't sit around forever waiting for my children to decide that I'm worthy of their visiting me. I've found someone who loves and likes me.*)

Writing my thoughts is good therapy; I should do it more often. (*I guess I get lazy!*)

Life is so lovely right now. I do almost anything I wish, despite having some heart issues. My excellent cardiologist keeps me in line! And I plan to have a spur removed before the trip; I certainly don't want that to be a distraction in Hawaii.

Otherwise, I stay busy, especially during the Christmas season. Other times, Jose and I make and sell tamales, such fun.

Beyond Jose's excellent company, I talk to Rosie and Carole, two of my great friends. I also spend time with my loved sister Tillie. Almost every day, like clockwork, we go to Walmart. You never know what you'll see there! We always have a wonderful time there.

My daughter Annette comes by the house off and on; of course, we do fun things together. I am grateful to have her in my life.

I guess that's it for today. I will write again soon. My fiancé is already in bed, so I'm heading that way. 'Til next time.

December 14, 2021

As you may already know, I recently found my dear husband, Jose Abreo Acosta. We got married on December 3, 2021, in Hawaii. (*Stephen and Annette were there for the celebration. They loved Hawaii and plan to return soon.*)

While in Oahu, we traveled all over the island; it was truly remarkable. One of the unique blessings of the trip was meeting Jose's sister-in-law, Tutu, as well as his friends Jay and Kathy Jung. We stayed at their house for two days.

The entire experience was more than I could have imagined. Jose and I had so much fun; I've never had that much fun with any of my former husbands. I am shocked at Jose's care and attention to my needs. I am thrilled and blessed. And his family is a complete joy.

That's all for now. Will write again soon.

Wow, it's been a while since I last wrote, but here I am! Oddly, I'm at home alone today. Jose is off working for DoorDash. It's hard to describe everything about Jose; he's the man I have been looking for all my life. His love for me is so visible, and he takes such good care of me. His presence makes me feel safer in this crazy world.

I have been going back to school again, but things are so much different than when I was younger. I struggle to get out of bed and out the door by 6:00 a.m. I don't move as quickly as I used to, and it takes me a long time to get dressed. My health isn't what I'd like it to be. I struggle with Diabetes. Insulin shots aren't helping as much as I hoped. Nevertheless, I will not give up. I'll win this battle!

My time is mostly my own; I do whatever I choose. Lazy mornings with Jose are so wonderful. I love how he makes and gets me coffee every morning. (*Sadly, my stomach isn't as durable as it once was. I have problems with my entire digestive system. It's frustrating.*)

Financially, things are good. I have enough to cover the utilities for the house and the annual property taxes. Jose helps with expenses, too. He pays half of my truck payment, as well as my water, cable, and cell phone bills. Assisting with those items represents a considerable amount of financial support. We manage to find time for entertainment in our area. I especially love places I've never seen before.

Jose loves Hawaii, where we got married. I think he'd move back there, but I like it right where I am in Canyon Lake. I am so fortunate to have gotten this house through Camilo, who was a wonderfully giving person. May he rest in peace. I know how blessed I was to meet Jose after losing Camilo. After we started talking, love was just around the corner.

As I have mentioned before, I've known Jose's family for decades. I've always been close to his mom, Fe Acosta. Fe and her sister, Gloria, were wonderful people, as was the entire family. Efrain Abreo, my former brother-in-law, married my sister, Tillie Escamilla Abreo. Efrain always made me laugh.

My family situation, particularly my daughters, has improved dramatically; both girls are talking to me. I'm close to Nina (Lovato-Rangel) and Thelma Lynn (Leyva Erskine). Thelma texts me a lot. Annette (Leyva Wagner) is the daughter who cares so much about me. She's my angel, and I love her most. And, as always, I am close to my sister Tillie. She's been right beside me since the day I was born, seventy-two years ago!

These days, I find myself reflecting on all the years that have passed. I've always wanted so much for myself. I dreamed of being a judge, a train engineer, or a physician's assistant (PA). Yet, I became a nurse. In some ways, I was getting greedy regarding everything I wanted out of life. But, thankfully, I'm happy. I've witnessed numerous illnesses and provided attentive care to everyone assigned to me.

Some improved, while others passed away. (*I lost Dr. Rabinowitz, an excellent cardiologist, two years ago.*)

I love writing in my book; I could do it all day. Writing allows me to re-experience all the good and not-so-good in my life. Additionally, I have been fortunate enough to explore a variety of interests, including swimming, sewing, crocheting, writing poetry, cooking a range of dishes, and taking road trips near and far.

January 15, 2025

Today will be the last time I write in this book. This entire process, spanning approximately thirty years, has been a wonderful outlet for me to express my deepest thoughts and memories. I pray it will be of benefit to all who read it.

My initial final thoughts revolve around my nursing career. It all started at Hondo Memorial Hospital, where I began a nurse's aide program. At the time, I was unable to complete the program due to the processing of my first divorce in 1999.

Shortly after, Dr. Ziegenbalg offered me a job as an Office Nurse. His experienced, well-qualified nurse, originally from Africa, trained me. I learned everything possible from her until she stopped working in 1973.

I worked for Dr. Ziegenbalg for four years. Sadly, he was killed in an automobile accident. Thereafter, I worked at Richard's World of Bargains, a clothing store. After five years there, I bought the store and renamed it Lydia's Apparel.

At the time, I was married to Salvador Dominguez Leyva. Our marriage was troubled and infused with constant fighting. Eventually, Salvador and I divorced; it was my second. My third husband was Albert Joe Lovato, a man I have talked about at great length in this book.

While married to Albert, I attended college at the San Antonio School of Nursing. I graduated in 1984.

My first post-graduate job was at Universal City Emergency Clinic. Soon after, I began working with Dr. Carlos Campos, who was a medical resident physician at the time. We worked together for ten years (1985-1995) at McKenna Hospital, specifically in the Labor and Delivery department, starting in 1984.

Thereafter, I worked at San Antonio's Southeast Baptist Memorial Hospital from 1997 to 1998. Initially, I worked in the Medical and Surgical department, then moved to Labor and Delivery. Two years later, I transferred to WellMed's Geriatrics department, a nursing area that I enjoyed until retirement fifteen years later.

Nursing was a remarkable career. In total, I served as a nurse for forty-four years. I saw it all; helped save lives and worked alongside some wonderful people. Retirement is wonderful, but I miss hands-on nursing.

Life has not been easy. I raised my children to the best of my ability and loved them with all my heart long before they were born. Now, life is nearing its end.

This book, or life journal, was written for those who choose to read it as an attempt to understand me and my heritage more clearly.

Although many people disagree, I believe my childhood years were excellent. I loved and liked my parents. They loved each other deeply, and they loved us.

As I became an adult, wife, and mother, I strived to live an honest, loving life. From the day my children were born, I have been forever proud of them through thick and thin. They are respectful humans who enjoy life.

I've been married four times, twice to the same man. My present husband is the best, most caring husband I've ever had. I love him deeply.

Again, life hasn't been easy. Nevertheless, I treasure all that I've experienced in life, the good and the bad.

I love my children forever and wish them the best this life can offer.

God's blessings to you all and always, always ... pray to our Father. I pray that God will heal my diabetes. That may or may not happen. Only God knows what's ahead. Regardless of what comes, I will always be by your side, and you will forever be in my heart.

Love and kisses,
Mommy (Ayda Lydia Escamilla)

APPENDIX
Documents and Photographs

- National Nurses' Day Memorial 2025;
  by daughter Annette Marie Leyva Wagner

- "My Nursing Career" – Essay; Ayda Lydia
  Escamilla, edited by Michael Marcades, PhD.

- ESCAMILLA Ancestral History

- Photographs and Additional Documents

NATIONAL NURSE'S DAY
May 6, 2025
In Honor of Ayda Lydia Escamilla

by daughter Annette Marie Leyva Wagner

Over the centuries, millions of dedicated nurses worldwide have provided meticulous care for patients suffering from every conceivable malady in every imaginable setting: local and state-affiliated hospitals, doctors' offices and clinics, emergency rooms, public and private schools, short-term and long-term care nursing homes and private residences, bullet and bomb riddled battlefields, and more. The kind, patient touch and care of nurses have always been a gift to humanity.

Among those caring career nurses is my mother, Ayda Lydia Escamilla. Today, I honor her. Below is an overview of her decades-long career of sacrifice.

- 1968-69; studied nursing at Hondo Memorial Hospital

- 1969; employed as a nurse for Dr. Ernest Ziegenbalg, Castroville, Texas
- 1980; completed General Education Diploma
- 1982; attended Licensed Vocational Nursing School at Nebraska Western College
- 1982; transferred to the San Antonio School of Nursing while employed by Dr. Park in Universal City, Texas
- 1984; graduated from San Antonio School of Nursing as a Licensed Vocational Nurse
- 1984-1994; employed as a nurse for Dr. Carlos Campos, New Braunfels, Texas
- 1991-93; employed as a nurse at McKenna Memorial Hospital, New Braunfels, Texas
- 1992; received IV Certification
- 1994-96; employed as a nurse with Dr. Ernesto Guerra and Dr. Charles Rabinowitz
- 1996; attended Palo Alto College, San Antonio, Texas
- 1998; employed as a nurse in Labor and Delivery at Baptist Memorial Hospital, San Antonio
- 1999-2014; employed as a nurse for Dr. Valentine Salcher at WellMed Medical Clinic
- 2014-2017; reinstated LVN license and started attending Austin Community College's Continuing Education Department

—

"How about them apples!" – Annette Marie Leyva Wagner

MY NURSING CAREER
Sociology 1301-296 – Spring Flex Essay
Edited by Michael Marcades, PhD

I came from a very poor but respectful family in Hondo, Texas. By the age of seventeen, I was engaged and looking forward to a Catholic Church wedding. Father Silverman, our priest at the time, refused to officiate due to my age until I went through three months of supervised counseling with my husband-to-be. At the end of the counseling with Father Silverman, he agreed to allow marriage. My wedding was beautiful.

My decision to enter nursing was influenced by the accidental death of my father-in-law, Bentura Leyva. Initially, Bentura's death seemed to have been caused by choking on food during a meal. However, it should be noted that he also had diabetes. So, his death could have been the result of his choking on food or a Diabetes-related seizure. Regardless, the event motivated my pursuit of nursing; I wanted to help people live healthier lives.

Overall, I greatly enjoyed my nursing career. Nevertheless, I reached a point when I wanted to retire but was unable to do so. Consequently, I decided to pursue my General Education Diploma (GED) and obtain my nursing license through the San Antonio School of Nursing.

Thereafter, I was employed as a nurse in the obstetrics and labor and delivery departments at McKenna Hospital, followed by Baptist Health System Hospital. Beyond OB, I was also drawn to medical-surgical departments, which allowed me to continue providing care for diabetes patients.

I have been fortunate to have completed forty-four years in nursing. I enjoyed every minute along the way. And I have consistently pursued continuing education to expand my nursing skills.

I have always been drawn to help patients with diabetes, a disease that plagues millions worldwide. Professionally, I am fascinated by the adverse impacts of this disease, especially on pregnant women. My interest in diabetes redirected some of my nursing aspirations.

Diabetes is a blood sugar level disorder that exists in several types, including Type 1, Type 2, mellitus, brittle, bronze, gestational, and insipidus diabetes. Though symptoms vary according to type, excessive urine excretion is particularly common to most diabetes types. (*I have spent extensive time studying diabetes mellitus.*)

Pregnant women tend to have either mellitus or gestational diabetes, the latter of which is found in women who have increased blood sugar levels *solely during pregnancy*. Conversely, women can also contract diabetes mellitus long before or during pregnancy.

Diabetes mellitus is a metabolic disorder in which the human body loses the ability to oxidize and utilize carbohydrates because of disturbances in the normal insulin mechanism. Such disruption leads to abnormalities in protein and fat metabolism.　Fat oxidation is accelerated in diabetes; therefore, there is an accumulation of fat metabolism end products in the blood, plus the development of ketosis symptoms, acidosis, and potential coma.

Factors leading to disturbances of the standard insulin mechanism and the onset of diabetes mellitus include:

- insufficient production of insulin from the beta cells of the Islands of Langerhans in the pancreas,
- an increase in the requirements by the tissue cells, or a decrease in the effectiveness of insulin due to one or more insulin antagonists that can deactivate insulin.

Any of the above-listed factors may produce the symptoms of diabetes mellitus.　Because diabetes prevents proper carbohydrate utilization in the blood, patients remain nutritionally malnourished, regardless of the amount of food consumed.　The accumulation of unused glucose causes physical weakness, extensive fatigue, and a "spilling over" of sugar in the urine.　(*Untreated diabetes patients are highly susceptible to various infections.*)

Prolonged, severe diabetes patients, those with excessively high fat and glucose levels in the blood, may see increased damage to blood vessels, body tissues, and organs containing blood vessels.　The resultant poor blood circulation may be a factor leading to other complications, such as gangrene in the hands and feet.　Additionally, there may be sustained damage to the heart and kidneys, vision abnormalities, or nervous system deterioration. Other advanced diabetes symptoms include hyperglycemia (*abnormally high glucose levels in the blood*), glycosuria (*excessive sugar in the urine or blood*), polyuria (*persistently excessive flow of urine*), polyphagia or hyperphagia (*excessive or pathological desire to eat*), polydipsia (*excessive, prolonged thirst*), and general physical weakness.

Diabetes testing methods include urine sugar level analysis (eventually superseded by more effective methods), a fasting blood sugar test, a hemoglobin A1c (HbA1c) test, or a glucose tolerance test. All diabetes tests analyze the human body's ability to produce insulin, a hormone that helps convert glucose into energy.

Treatments* for diabetes depend on disease severity, patient age, and exhibited symptoms. Primarily, diabetes is controlled through diet modification**, physical exercise, oral medications***, and/or insulin administration.

Education: Patient education is a crucial aspect of treatment. As with any disease, patients must understand the nature of their disorder and their role in managing it.

**Dietary modification*: Although varied among physicians, the 1600-calorie diet is one of the most prescribed diet modifications. Extensive information about every aspect of diabetes and diet modifications is available from The Diabetes Association, 1660

Duke Street, Alexandria, VA 22314. 1-800-DIABETES, http://www.diabetes.org.

****Oral medications: In recent years, oral antidiabetic medications have undergone significant evolution. Presently, two of the most effective oral medications include Actos and Rezulin, though the latter was taken off the market due to adverse liver function issues. (See the 2000 Physicians' Desk Reference [PDR] for a complete diabetes-related oral medication listing.)*

Generally, diabetes-related disorder complications can be divided into two categories: emergency conditions and long-term conditions. One such emergency condition is known as insulin shock. Initially, people experiencing insulin shock are instructed to seek immediate treatment at an emergency room or promptly call their primary care doctor. Over time, patients may learn to manage the shock event by consuming a form of sugar, such as sweetened orange juice, a small amount of raw sugar, or hard candy. If the latter efforts do not end the shock event, patients should take additional actions as described above.

Insulin shocks occur for various reasons. These short-term shock disturbances may be brought on by patients not adhering to dietary guidelines, careless administration of insulin, infections, or random emotional and physical events. Long-term events are often triggered by poor fat metabolism, which can contribute to the development of atherosclerosis. In such cases, the coronary arteries may be damaged, potentially leading to heart disease, or the peripheral arteries may be damaged, causing poor circulation in the lower extremities. Additionally, one may experience sclerosis of the renal capillaries, which can cause nerve damage.****

> ****Much of the above-listed information was taken from the second edition of The Encyclopedia and Dictionary of Medicine, Nursing, and Allied Health.

Unknown to many, early prevention actions for diabetes are possible and can be quite effective, even if an individual's family has a history of the disease. Two of the most effective preventive actions include adhering to recommended weight guidelines and engaging in regular physical activity.

I recommend that people stay on top of their health by having regular doctor visits and annual physical examinations. Procrastination kills; don't wait until it's too late for simple diabetes treatments and associated medications to save your life. (*Note: All patients should be proactive when it comes to personal health, particularly as it relates to diabetes. Technically speaking, there is no "in-between" diagnosis; you either have a diagnosis or you don't. Keep an eye on patient charts and learn the "secret" coding. The "secret" superbill CPK code, 250.0, denotes that you have been diagnosed with diabetes.*)

Sadly, my mother was diabetic; so far, I have not experienced related symptoms. I hope that doesn't change!

Final Reflections

Nursing, though a deeply rewarding career for me, is not for everyone. Success as a nurse requires courage, willpower, knowledge and comprehension, a desire to constantly learn and improve skills, patience, kindness, and respect for those under your care.

As for me, I believe that I made the right career choice. And I wish my children had followed in my footsteps.

In closing, I acknowledge that this class, along with all my nursing courses and clinicals, has challenged and advanced my personal development as a nurse.

Ayda Lydia Escamilla

Graduation from the San Antonio School of Nursing as a Licensed Vocational Nurse - 1984

ESCAMILLA
Ancestral History
Lands of Origin: Italy, Portugal, Spain, Mexico, Central
Mexico (Aztecs), United States of America (Texas)

AYDA LYDIA ESCAMILLA / b. June 20, 1950 / Hondo,
Texas

> Marriages: Salvador Dominguez Leyva, Albert
> Joe Lovato, John Bermea, Camillo
> G. Caranza, Jose Abreo Acosta
>
> Children: Annette Marie Leyva Wagner,
> Salvador Leyva Jr., Thelma Lynn
> Leyva Erskine, Ada Stephanie Leyva
> Ingram, Nina Ruby Lovato Rangel
>
> Grandchildren: Kathryn Marie Correa, Jesse
> Alexander Cortez, Rey Leyva,
> Hannah Saki Leyva, Taylor Nicole
> Erskine, Bailey Scott Erskine, Elijah
> Rames Ingram, Ruby Olivia Rangel,
> Mateo Isidro Rangel IV, Benjamin
> Albert Rangel
>
> Great-Grandchildren: Jesse Ryan Cortez, Elaina
> Martinez Cortez, Zaeden Charles
> Hale, Orion Leo Serna, Marina
> Elzbeth Erskine, Elanor Erskine

PARENTS

> Mother: Maria Ysabel Muniz / b. December
> 20, 1911 - d. August 5, 1995
> Origin: Masapil, Zacatecas, Mexico
> Burial: Hondo, Texas.

Note: Maria Ysabel had one sister, Bonifacia Bivero Benavides, who married Isidro Benavides. Cuco, Abraham, Victoria Elodia, and Lucia Benavides, all born in Hondo, Texas.

Additionally, there is one first cousin, Ma Ramona Rivera Ybarra, who married Hilaro Ybarra. Maria Ysabel moved to Hondo, Texas, in 1924 with her mother, Ma Eufrosina, due to Pancho Villa's retaliations.

Father: Luis Lopez Escamilla / b. Oct 13, 1900 - d. March 16, 1966
Origin: Zaragoza, Coahuila, Mexico
Burial: Hondo, Texas.

Children: Luis Fidencio Muniz Escamilla, Juan Muniz Escamilla, Efrain Muniz Escamilla, Clotilde Escamilla, Elia Juliet Escamilla, Sofia Escamilla, Julio Muniz Escamilla, Oscar Muniz Escamilla, Ayda Lydia Escamilla, Belia Guadalupe Escamilla.

Note: Maria Ysabel lost one other child at birth due to surgical complications.

UNITED STATES DEPARTMENT OF JUSTICE
IMMIGRATION AND NATURALIZATION SERVICE

Form approved.
Budget Bureau No. 43-R082.9.

ORIGINAL
(To be retained
by Clerk of Court)

UNITED STATES OF AMERICA

PETITION FOR NATURALIZATION

Filed under ___ sect 316-a

No. 2 6 3 7 9

To the Honorable
The _____ U.S.District _____ Court of _ West. Dist. of Texas _ San Antonio, Tex.

This petition for naturalization, hereby made and filed, respectfully shows:

(1) My full, true, and correct name is _ Luis Lopez Escamilla _
(2) My present place of residence is _ 418 15th St. Hondo _ Medina _ Texas _
(3) My occupation is _ retired _
(4) I was born on _ Oct. 12, 1900 _ in _ Zafagoza Coah., Mexico _
(5) My personal description is as follows: Sex _ male _ complexion _ med _, color of eyes _ brown _, color of hair _ gray _,
height _ 5 _ feet _ 6 _ inches, weight _ 145 _ pounds, visible distinctive marks _ blemish lft temple _
country of which I am a citizen, subject, or national _ Mexico _
(6) I am _ married; the name of my wife or husband is _ Isabel nee Muniz _ we were
married on _ Nov. 21, 1927 _ at _ Hondo Texas _ he or she was born
at _ Zacatecas _ on _ Dec. 20th 1912 _, and entered the United
States at _ Eagle Pass, Texas _ on _ Oct. 15, 1919 _ for permanent residence in the United States
and now resides at _ with me _ and was naturalized on _ Sept. 2, 1965 _
at _ San Antonio, Texas _ certificate No. _ 103 _ or became a citizen by _

(7a) (If petition is filed under section 319 (a), Immigration and Nationality Act.) I have resided in the United States in marital union with my United States citizen spouse for at least 3 years immediately preceding the date of filing this petition for naturalization, and have been physically present in the United States at least half of that time.

(7b) (If petition is filed under section 319 (b), Immigration and Nationality Act.) My husband or wife is a citizen of the United States, is in the employment of the Government of the United States, or of an American institution of research recognized as such by the Attorney General of the United States, or an American firm or corporation engaged in whole or in part in the development of foreign trade and commerce of the United States, or a subsidiary thereof, or of a public international organization in which the United States participates by treaty or statute, or is engaged solely as a missionary by a religious denomination or by an interdenominational mission organization having a bona fide organization within the United States, and such husband or wife is regularly stationed abroad in such employment. I intend in good faith upon naturalization to live abroad with my spouse and to resume my residence within the United States immediately upon termination of such employment abroad.

(8) I have _ nine _ living children.

(9) My lawful admission for permanent residence in the United States was at _ Eagle Pass, Texas _
under the name of _ Luis Escamilla _ on _ March 8, 1919 _
on the _ toll bridge _

(10) Since my lawful admission for permanent residence I have not been absent from the United States, for a period or periods of 6 months or longer, except as follows:

DEPARTED FROM THE UNITED STATES			RETURNED TO THE UNITED STATES		
PORT	DATE (Month, day, year)	VESSEL OR OTHER MEANS OF CONVEYANCE	PORT	DATE (Month, day, year)	VESSEL OR OTHER MEANS OF CONVEYANCE
		none			

(11) It is my intention in good faith to become a citizen of the United States and to renounce absolutely and entirely all allegiance and fidelity to any foreign prince, potentate, state, or sovereignty of whom or which at this time I am a subject or citizen. (12) It is my intention to reside permanently in the United States. (13) I am not and have not been for a period of at least 10 years immediately preceding the date of this petition a member of or affiliated with any organization proscribed by the Immigration and Nationality Act or any section, subsidiary, branch, affiliate or subdivision thereof nor have I during such period believed in, advocated, engaged in or performed any of the acts or activities prohibited by that Act. (14) I am able to read, write and speak the English language (unless exempted therefrom). (15) I am, and have been during all the periods required by law, a person of good moral character, attached to the principles of the Constitution of the United States and well disposed to the good order and happiness of the United States. I am willing, if required by law, to bear arms on behalf of the United States, to perform noncombatant service in the Armed Forces of the United States, and to perform work of national importance under civilian direction (unless exempted therefrom). (16) I have resided continuously in the United States since _ March 8, 1919 _ and continuously in the State in which this petition is made for the term of 6 months at least immediately preceding the date of this petition and I have been physically present in the United States for at least one-half of the _ 5 _ year period immediately preceding the date of this petition. (17) I have _ not _ heretofore made petition for naturalization No. _____
on _____ at _____ in
the _____ Court, and such petition was denied by that Court for the following reasons and causes, to-wit:

(18) Attached hereto and made a part of this, my petition for naturalization, are the affidavits of at least two verifying witnesses required by law.
(19) Wherefore I, your petitioner for naturalization, pray that I may be admitted a citizen of the United States of America, and that my name be changed to
_ none _. I, aforesaid petitioner, do swear (affirm) that I know the contents of this petition for naturalization subscribed by me, and that the same are true to the best of my knowledge and belief, and that this petition is signed by me with my full, true name: SO HELP ME GOD.

ALIEN REGISTRATION NO. _ A3 448 680 _

(signature)

FORM N-405
(Rev. 11-1-52)

Naturalization Petition: Luis Lopez Escamilla and Maria Ysabel Muniz, San Antonio, Texas, 1965

GRANDPARENTS:

Maternal:	Hilario Muniz / b. 1881 - d. 1911 Origin: Masapil, Zacatecas, Mexico Burial: Masapil, Zacatecas, Mexico Maria Eufrosina Rivera / b. January 1, 1883 - d. August 14, 1924 Origin: Masapil, Zacatecas, Mexico Burial: Hondo, Texas
Paternal:	Jose Cristino Jesus de la Merced Griego Escamilla / b. December 25, 1835 - d. January 26, 1940 Origin: San Antonio, Mexico Burial: Hondo, Texas Maria del Pilar Carmen Lopez Perez Escamilla / b. 1835 - d. February 23, 1936 Origin: San Antonio, Mexico / Zaragoza, Coahuila, Mexico Burial: Devine, Texas
Children:	Polecarpio Lopez Escamilla, Maria Ines Escamilla (from Del Rio, Texas), Julio Lopez Escamilla, Jose Lopez Escamilla, Maria Rita Lopez Escamilla (married Jesus Valdez - Eagle Pass, Texas), Maria Conselo Lopez Escamilla (married Isidro Garza - Hondo, Texas), Maria Sarita Lopez Escamilla (married Manurel Gonzales (from San Antonio, Texas), Maria Irene Lopez Escamilla

(married Jose Galindo from Hondo, Texas), Felimon Lopez Escamilla (marriage unknown), Guadalupe Lopez Escamilla (marriage unknown, lived in Piedras Negras Coahuila, Mexico, had two sons (Guadalupe Escamilla - Mexico-based lawyer), and Hector Escamilla (San Antonio-based Endocrinologist / Cardiologist.

GREAT-GRANDPARENTS

Maternal: Juanita Rivera / b. 1863 - d. 1923, and Unidentified Aztec Indian Male
Origin: Marsapil, Zacatecas, Mexico
Burial: Marsapil, Zacatecas, Mexico
Paternal: Petronilo Escamilla and Juanita Refugio Escamilla
Origin: San Antonio, Mexico
Burial: San Antonio, Texas
   Note: Juanita died by public hanging in front of Santa Rosa Plaza during the Alamo War (1835). Thereafter, she was piled up with other victims and cremated.

GREAT-GREAT-GRANDPARENTS

Maternal: Unidentified / 1820?
Origin: Spain / Mexico
Burial: Mexico

Paternal: Jose Petronilo Ysaac Sacramento
                Escamilla Lopez and Conception
                Escamilla / 1560
                Origin: Mexico
                Burial: Mexico
                        Note: Petronilo Escamilla
                        was in San Antonio, Mexico,
                        during the Alamo / moved to
                        Zaragosa, Coahuila, Mexico,
                        with three sons (Refugio,
                        Luciano, and Cristino) / later
                        returned to San Antonio,
                        Texas, after the Battle of the
                        Alamo.   He was buried at
                        San Fernando Cemetery #1,
                        San Antonio, Texas.

DOCUMENTS
AND PHOTOGRAPHS

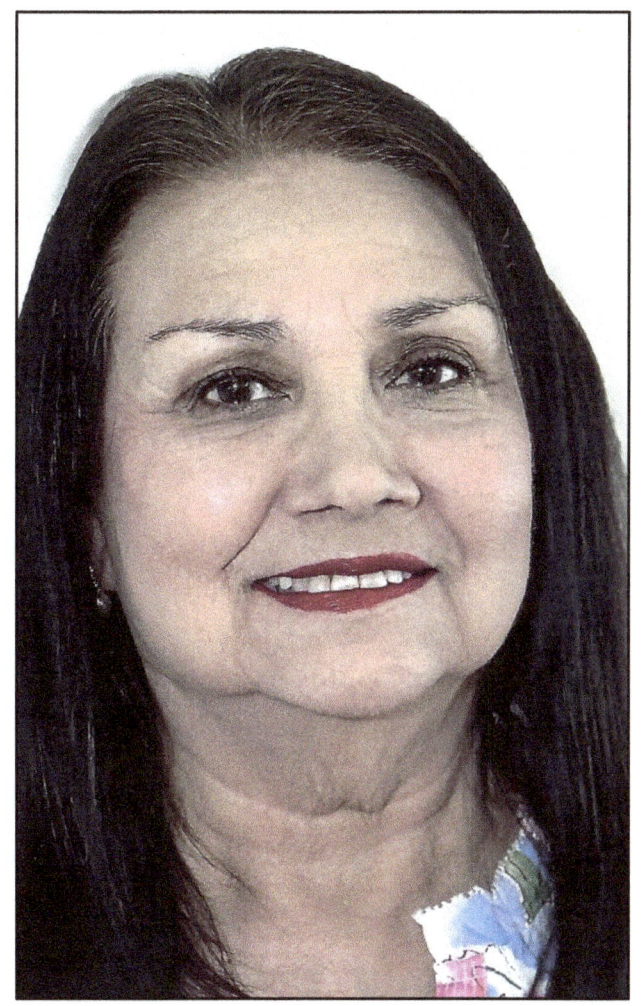

AYDA LYDIA ESCAMILLA
June 2025
Canyon Lake, Texas

Parents' Wedding:
Luis Lopez and Maria Ysabel Escamilla
November 19, 1927 – Hondo, Texas

Liber Matrimoniorum in Ecclesia

No.	Nomina Contrahentium	Tempus Matrimonii			Tempus et Ecclesia Baptismi vel locus Nativitatis Sponsi	Parentes Sponsi
		Annus	Mensis	Dies		
1	Sponsi *Manuel Duran*				31 years Mexico	Luz Duran
	Sponsa *Maria Jesus Salazar*	1827	October	22		Refugia Jimenez
2	*Juan Duran*				33 years Mexico	Luz Duran
	Sponsa *Isabel Salinas*	1927	Oct.	22		Refugia Jimenez
3	*Pedro Valdez*				25 years Mexico	Victoriano Valdez
	Augustina Arriaga	1927	Oct.	25		Carla Hernandez
4	Sponsus *Tomas Orozco*				March 1905 Castroville	Juan Orozco
	Sponsa *Eufemia Gonzalez*	1927	Oct.	25		Delfina Diaz
5	Sponsus *Manuel Gurriola*				Mex. 27 yrs.	Cristobal Gurriola
	Sponsa *Ramona Garza*	1927	14	Nov.		Maria Renela
6	Sponsus *Luis Escamilla*				Mex. 22 yrs.	Cristino Escamilla
	Sponsa *Isabel Muniz*	1927	19	Nov.		Maria Pilar Lopez
7	*Pablo Rocha*				Mex. 25 yrs.	Gonzalo Rocha
	Sponsa *Juanita Valdez*	1927	23	Nov.		Remiria Jarne
8	*Alfredo Santos*				Mex. Apr. 25, 1906	Jose Leon Santos
	Sponsa *Consuela Lopez*	1927	Nov.	27		Adela Chiciana
9	Sponsus *Simon Flores*				35 yrs. Mex.	Manuel Flores
	Sponsa *Cicuicia Alvarez*	1927	Dec.	26		Pilar Salazar
10	Sponsus *Heliberto Dominguez*				20 yrs. Mex.	Ricardo Dominguez
	Sponsa *Ramona Reyes*	1927	Dec.	31		Refugia Reyes
11	Sponsus *Salome Ruiz*				27 yrs. Elmendorf	Braulio Ruiz
	Leona Martinez	1927	Dec.	14		Concepcion Stanley
12	Sponsae *Fernando P*					

Catholic Church Marriage Registry
for Luis Lopez Escamilla and Isabel Muniz
St. John's Catholic Church, Hondo, Texas
November 19, 1927
Godparents: Cristinio Escamilla
and Maria Pilar Lopez.

Ayda's
Grandmother:
Maria del Pilar
Carmen Lopez
Perez Escamilla;
Ayda's father:
Luis Lopez
Escamilla

c. 1907
Zaragosa,
Coahuila,
Mexico.

Ayda's
Grandmother:
Maria
Eufrosina
Rivera

c. 1920

Hondo, Texas

Ayda Lydia Escamilla
b. June 20, 1950

9 months old
Hondo, Texas

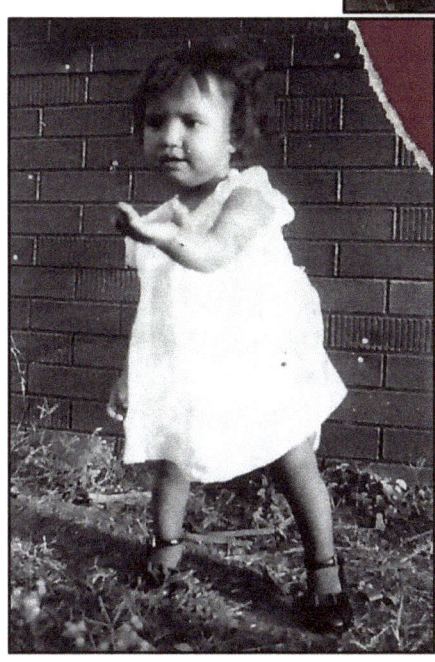

2 years old
Hondo, Texas

Ayda Lydia Leyva
17 years old
Wedding – Hondo, Texas
August 1967

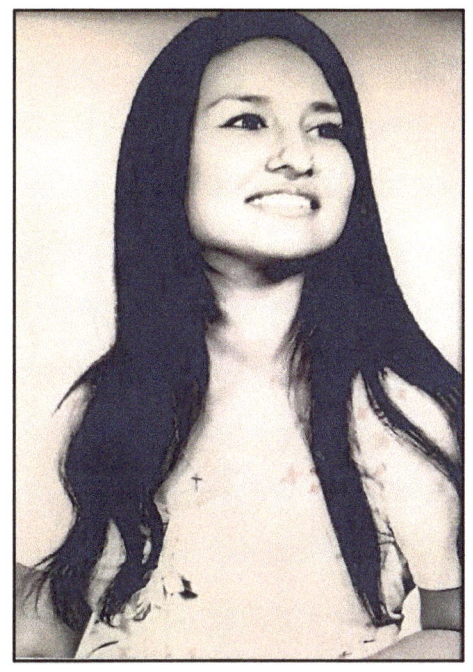

Ayda Lydia Leyva
23 years old
Hondo, Texas
1973

Ayda Lydia Lovato
54 years old
Live Oak, Texas
2004

Ayda Lydia Escamilla
Native Texan
Resident of Live Oak, Hondo, Canyon Lake

Courthouse
Hondo, Texas

Canyon Lake, Texas

San
Antonio,
Riverwalk

Ayda's Children:
Annette Marie Leyva Wagner, Salvador Leyva Jr.,
Thelma Lynn Leyva Erskine, Ada Stephanie Leyva
Ingram, Nina Ruby Lovato Rangel

Wedding
December 3, 2021, Honolulu, Hawaii

Jose Abreo Acosta and
Ayda Lydia Escamilla

Kawaikui Beach Park
Honolulu, Hawaii

Wedding Ceremony
with Justice of the Peace
Honolulu, Hawaii

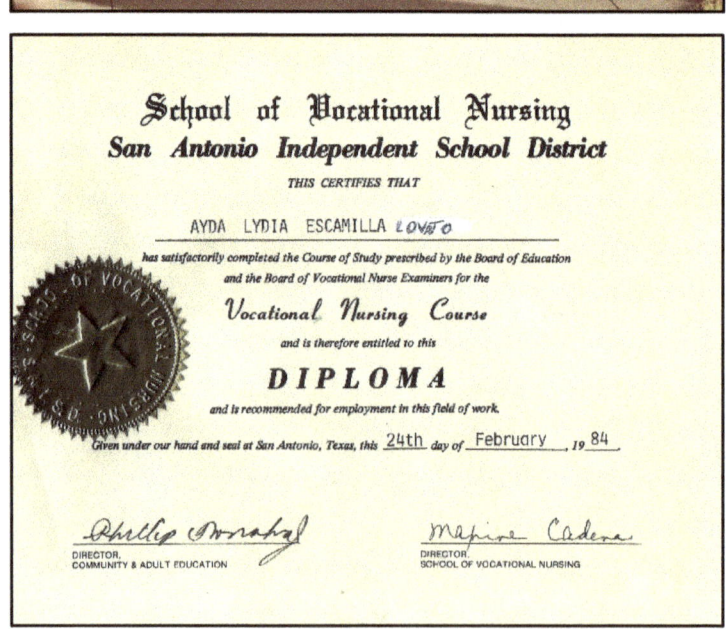

School of Vocational Nursing

San Antonio Independent School District

THIS CERTIFIES THAT

AYDA LYDIA ESCAMILLA LOVETO

has satisfactorily completed the Course of Study prescribed by the Board of Education
and the Board of Vocational Nurse Examiners for the

Vocational Nursing Course

and is therefore entitled to this

D I P L O M A

and is recommended for employment in this field of work.

Given under our hand and seal at San Antonio, Texas, this 24th day of February , 19 84

DIRECTOR,
COMMUNITY & ADULT EDUCATION

DIRECTOR,
SCHOOL OF VOCATIONAL NURSING

140

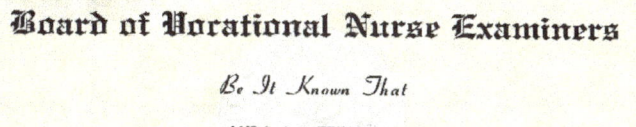

Board of Vocational Nurse Examiners

Be It Known That

AYDA L. ESCAMILLA

Having Given Satisfactory Evidence of Fitness and Having Fulfilled
All Other Requirements Prescribed By Law Is
Licensed To Practice As A
Licensed Vocational Nurse
In The State of Texas

In Witness Whereof, The Texas State
Board of Vocational Nurse Examiners
Grants This License No. 105135
Under Its Seal At Austin, Texas.
This 30th day of May, 1984.

_____ PRESIDENT

_____ SECRETARY

> **State of Texas Nursing License**

BAPTIST HEALTH SYSTEM
7930 Floyd Curl Drive · San Antonio, Texas 78229

Certificate of Successful Completion

This Confirms That

Ayda Bermea, LVN

successfully completed and is awarded 8.6 *contact hours for*

Neonatal Resuscitation Certification Course

presented in San Antonio, Texas

This the 5th *day of* March , 1998

The BAPTIST HEALTH SYSTEM, Provider #96-0573-B, is an approved provider of continuing education in Nursing by the Texas Nurses Association, which is accredited as an approver of continuing education in nursing by the American Nurses Credentialing Center's Commission on Accreditation. This approval meets Type I criteria for mandatory continuing education requirements toward relicensure as established by the Board of Nurse Examiners for the State of Texas.

> **Neonatal Resuscitation Certification**

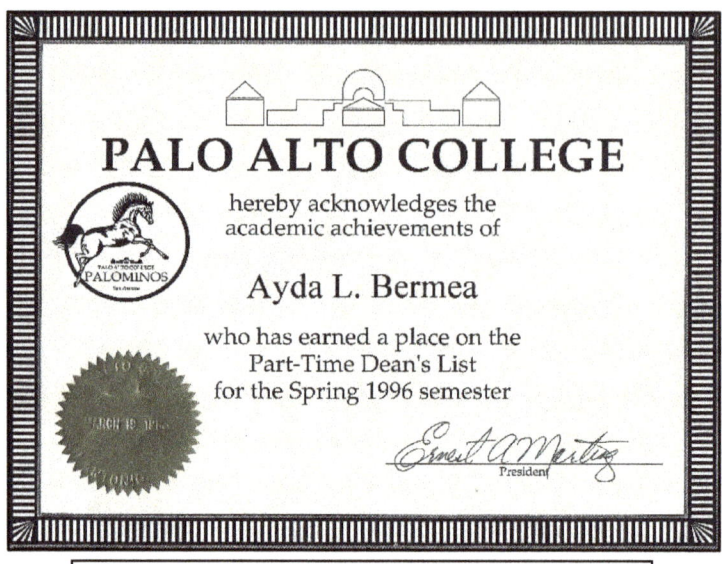

Palo Alto College Dean's List, 1996

State of Texas High School Graduation

WELLMED

We Gratefully Acknowledge

that

Ayda L. Lovato

has completed __3__ *years of service*

with WellMed Medical Management, Inc.

on this, the __21st__ *day of* December, 2001.

George M. Rajeev

George Rajeev, M.D.

WellMed Service Awards

WELLMED

We Gratefully Acknowledge

that

Ayda Lovato

has completed __5__ *years of service*

with WellMed Medical Management, Inc.

on this, the __21st__ *day of* December, 2003.

George M. Rajeev

George Rajeev, M.D.

Certificate of Achievement

awarded to:

AYDA LOVATO

Description of Achievements

November 1, 2004
Date

Signed

Achievement and Compliance Certifications

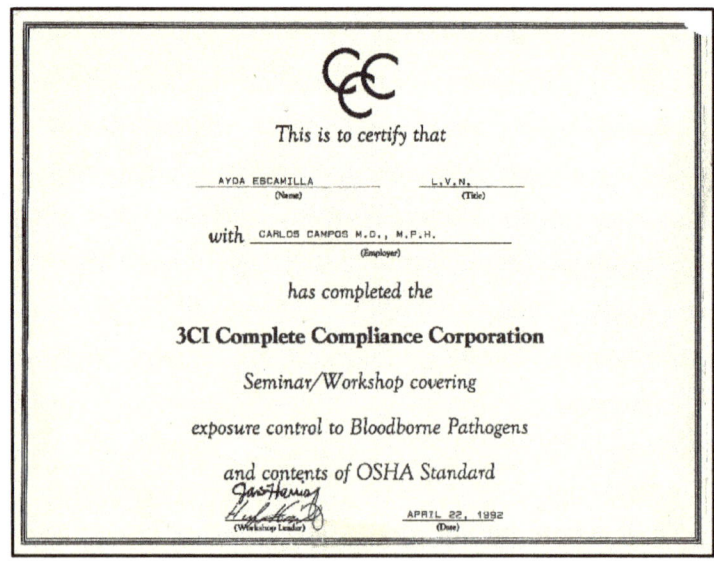

This is to certify that

AYDA ESCAMILLA (Name)   L.V.N. (Title)

with CARLOS CAMPOS M.D., M.P.H. (Employer)

has completed the

3CI Complete Compliance Corporation

Seminar/Workshop covering

exposure control to Bloodborne Pathogens

and contents of OSHA Standard

(Workshop Leader)   APRIL 22, 1992 (Date)

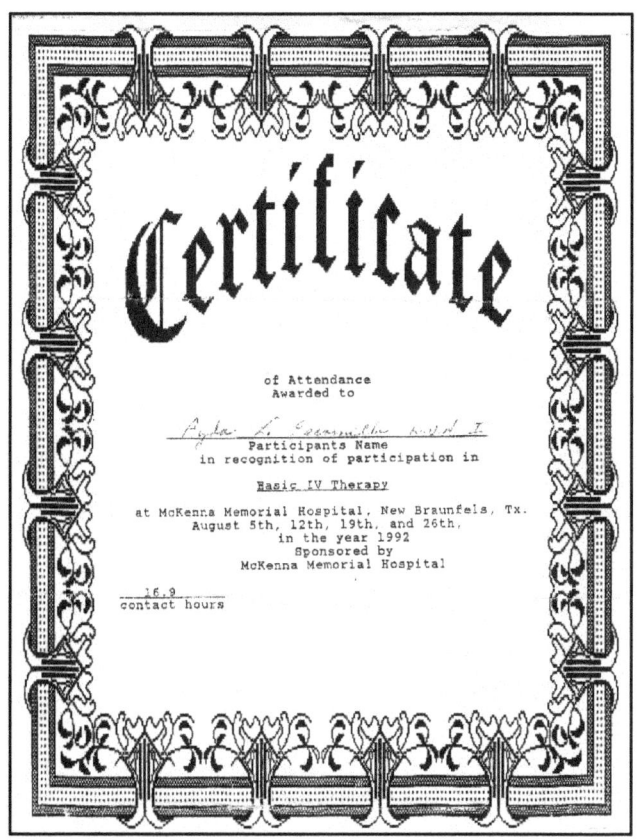

Certificate

of Attendance
Awarded to

Ayda L. Escamilla L.V.N. I
Participants Name

in recognition of participation in

Basic IV Therapy

at McKenna Memorial Hospital, New Braunfels, Tx.
August 5th, 12th, 19th, and 26th,
in the year 1992
Sponsored by
McKenna Memorial Hospital

16.9
contact hours

McKenna Memorial Hospital Basic IV Therapy
Certification and 2004 LVN License Renewal

BOARD OF VOCATIONAL NURSE EXAMINERS
333 GUADALUPE ST. TOWER 3 SUITE 400, AUSTIN, TX.78701
THE PERSON WHOSE NAME APPEARS HEREUNDER IS AUTHORIZED TO PRACTICE
AS A LICENSED VOCATIONAL NURSE UNDER THE LAWS OF THE STATE OF TEXAS.

L.V.N. NO.	TYPE	EXPIRATION DATE
105135	RENEWAL	06/30/04

AYDA L LOVATO
7913 FOREST CABIN
LIVE OAK, TX 78233

TERRIE HAIRSTON
EXECUTIVE DIRECTOR   SIGNATURE

www.ingramcontent.com/pod-product-compliance
Lightning Source LLC
Chambersburg PA
CBHW051207120626
46547CB00013B/1241